Antiques and Collectables Fact Book

ALL YOU NEED TO KNOW –
IN YOUR POCKET

Judith Miller

MILLER'S

Antiques & Collectables Fact Book
by Judith Miller

First published in Great Britain in 2008 by Miller's
a division of Mitchell Beazley,
imprints of Octopus Publishing Group Ltd,
2-4 Heron Quays, London E14 4JP
An Hachette Livre UK Company
www.hatchettelivre.co.uk
www.octopusbooks.co.uk

ISBN 978 184 533 4307

A CIP record of this book is available from the British
Library.

Set in Granjon.
Produced by Toppan Printing Co., (HK) Ltd.
Printed and bound in China

Publishing Manager Julie Brooke
Collectables Consultant Mark Hill
Design TJ Graphics
Sub-editors Katy Armstrong, John Parton, Sara Sturgess
Production Manager Peter Hunt
Indexer Christine Shuttleworth

Contents

Contents

Metalware

Clocks, Watches & Barometers

Other Antiques & Collectables

How to use this book

An Emile Gallé mahogany carved and inlaid display cabinet. c1905

Miller's Pocket Antiques & Collectables Fact Book has been devised to help both specialist and novice, collector and dealer. A great deal of research has been carried out to find the most useful facts to be included. Every effort has been made to reflect pieces which are in the market place and available to the antiques public – avoiding, wherever possible, museum pieces and the most expensive items. As a result, most facts included deal with 18th, 19th and 20th century pieces. For this we make no apology. From the many thousands of facts accumulated, we feel that those presented in this book most reflect buyers' needs.

The book is split into natural collecting areas. Accordingly, this is a book of solid facts, with charts, marks, dates, shapes and glossaries to assist with identification and dating. This is a book to take with you when you attend an auction, fair or go on a browse round antique shops.

It is important to state that marks alone cannot guarantee an item. This book cannot make you an instant antiques expert. What it does provide is the basic tools. To learn more you have to work – you have to educate your eye. You have to visit collections and museums; you have to spend time in antique shops; you have to ask specialists, and more than anything you have to handle the items. The joy of exploring the field of antiques and collectables is that it can take you a lifetime to discover and to learn. We all have to make mistakes but that is part of the learning process.

This book is designed to give you, ready at hand, the basic facts that we all find impossible instantly to remember.

The best advice on how to use this book is: make sure you have it with you all the time!

Judith Miller.

Factors affecting value

The problem of valuing antiques is a never-ending one, and one which we constantly address in producing Miller' s Antiques and Collectables Price Guides. A price can be affected by many factors, for example:

Condition

This is always an important factor and the best way to learn what a "perfect" piece should look like is to visit a museum. This is especially useful if one is looking to buy an expensive item of furniture, as you will see fine examples of wood, colour and patination. Perfect examples will, obviously, cost more. Damage and restoration is always to be regretted and the price must reflect this.

Desirability and rarity

Although a piece may be extremely rare, unless it is also desirable it will not necessarily command a high price. When a piece is extremely rare and desirable condition is not of prime importance.

Size

In general terms smaller pieces are favoured by the majority of buyers, with particular attention being paid to usability rather than to mere decoration. Thus, items such as bookcases, small tables and desks can fetch higher prices than a rarer but larger object that would not comfortably fit in the home.

Buyer's power

One can often be surprised at an auction by a piece selling for many times its estimated value. There can be several reasons for this. Perhaps the estimated price was incorrect. It is also possible that two or more people bid against each other until the sale price was well above the true value of the object.

Investment value

Another interesting point to bear in mind when buying items for the home (furniture being a prime example), is that once a new item has left the shop its value decreases dramatically. An antique should hold its value and in some cases the value of the piece will increase even though it is in use.

Public appeal

The fact that items or collections have been given exposure on television or in a specialist publication will arouse public interest, and substantially increase demand.

Location

As a large percentage of sales takes place from dealer to dealer, it is obvious that prices vary. It is also possible to pay more at a provincial auction than in a specialist shop in London or New York.

Learn as much as you can about your subject and beware something that looks too good to be true. It probably is!

Where to buy antiques

Antique Dealers: Shops, Markets and Fairs

Buying from an antique shop is probably where most people start. The entire spectrum is covered, from luxurious showrooms to the bric-a-brac dealer. There are two organisations which you will come across in Britain: BADA (British Antique Dealers Association) and LAPADA (London and Provincial Antique Dealers Association) whose members are bound by codes of practice. A good point to remember is that if you always ask for a full receipt you are covered by consumer protection legislation.

Other shops are harder to categorize; each has its own good buying points. An old dealer once told me that if you really know what you are doing, you should be able to find a bargain anywhere. I list below a couple of examples:

The pretty village shop is always worth visiting for two reasons: firstly the owner cannot possibly be an expert on every subject. Secondly, there is a chance the owner has had to buy stock in lots, some of which may not be saleable in that particular shop, and which he will be pleased to move on at a reasonable price.

The bric-a-brac or junk shop: I have made many good purchases from such shops but have also found that when they obtain a saleable but mediocre piece, it can be overpriced. Fairs, markets and fleamarkets range from the highly prestigious to the car boot fair in a field.

Auctions

Auctions rooms, if you are careful and knowledgeable can be an excellent source for all kinds of antiques. Don't be overawed by the jargon or by anything else. View the sale carefully and fix your price limit. Do try to stick to this and don't get carried away.

The internet

The internet has revolutionized the way antiques and collectables are bought and sold. Descriptions and photographs supplied on-line can be seen by buyers around the world. Providing the item is of a reasonable weight and size it can be delivered almost anywhere. Traditional auction houses post catalogues on websites and accept online bidding.

Selling

BADA and LAPADA dealers, also auction houses, particularly members of SOFAA (Society of Fine Art Auctioneers) are your best source of advice. Beware of the plausible, polite and seemingly generous people who knock on your door. "Knockers" are invariably up to no good. Always get a second opinion. The best advice is never to let them inside the house.

How to buy antiques

The main advice for anyone just starting to buy antiques is: do your research first. We have already discussed the many ways of buying antiques; what I want to deal with here is how to do it.

Antique Dealers

Do cultivate a "pet" dealer. Most specialists are fascinated with, and fascinating about, their subject and are willing to talk to an interested listener – who may well one day become a customer. But don't plague a dealer – especially when there is a potential customer in the shop. Don't be intimidated by any expert; everyone had to learn sometime. Don't, however, pretend to know more than you do. A dealer will know.

Do your research. The more museums you visit, books you read, auctions you go to, dealers you cultivate, the easier deciding what to buy will become. Buy **Miller's Antiques and Collectables Price Guides** every year to build up a photographic reference library and provide a ball-park figure of what to pay.

If you want to buy a specific type of antique go to an area where there are lots of specialist shops. You may find these shops charge slightly more, but if time is money – choice can be cheaper. Don't think that specialist dealers are necessarily more expensive. They know what to charge and although that can on occasion be more expensive, someone who is guessing may well charge more. You can ask a dealer what is his best price but if he won't shift, leave it.

Auctions

Auctions can be the most exciting place to buy antiques but the public do tend to be worried about attending them.

Firstly, an expensive item will not be knocked down to you if you scratch your nose! It is actually very difficult to attract the auctioneer's attention to take your initial bid.

Secondly, always view an auction properly. Obtain a catalogue and really examine the pieces in which you are interested. If there isn't a printed estimate, ask for a price guide. If a piece is reasonably expensive ask the auctioneer for advice about it. They can be very helpful, so don't be put off if you find an unhelpful auctioneer – every trade has them. Always check the condition of a piece carefully and remember that restoration can be very, very expensive. Now before you attend the auction set your own limit of how much you will pay and don't go above it. Remember that you have to add a "buyer's premium" onto the hammer price, which can be considerable.

Now the actual bid. It can be difficult as an unknown buyer to attract the auctioneer's attention. This is not a time for the faint-hearted. Wave your catalogue in the air and if

How to buy antiques

that doesn't work I'm afraid you have to shout "Sir" or "Madam". Once you have the auctioneer's attention, bid in a clear way. Where to start bidding is very much a personal decision. I start quite early on in the proceedings and hope to stop others bidding. Others leave it to the last minute! To stop shake your head or put your catalogue down.

You can, of course, leave a bid with the auction house; most have bidder's form. An auctioneer has a duty not to run up bids, but he can take bids "from the wall" up to the reserve. If you are nervous, leave your bids but still try to attend the auction, as there is nothing quite like the excitement. But don't bid above your limit, even though it is tempting to think that the next bid will succeed!

Be ready to pick up a bargain, but only if you remember the piece from the viewing. Some sales are poorly attended and bargains can abound. Don't feel that specialist auctions will automatically be more expensive. Some minor lots at important sales go cheaply.

Make arrangements for the auction house to accept your cheque if you are not paying cash. If you can't clear your lot or lots on the day you may have a storage charge. Most auction houses will arrange delivery but this can be expensive.

Auctions usually require you to register and obtain a bidding number, so do that before the auction starts. If this system is not in operation you need to shout out your name when a piece has been knocked down to you then fill in a form with your address etc. Obtain this from a member of staff.

Most people have heard stories about dealers' rings which supposedly control auctions. In my experience this is not a problem. The auctioneer has a responsibility to give the vendor advice on a sensible reserve. If some dealers have grouped together and agreed not to bid against each other it is the vendor who suffers, not the bidders. So ignore it.

The internet

Dealers, auction houses and online auctions are all potential hunting grounds. Read descriptions carefully and ask plenty of questions, particularly regarding condition. When you have purchased a piece you value, no matter how small, make a point of following this procedure:

1. Photograph it; a digital image is perfect.
2. Write a full description in a book kept for the purpose, with date of purchase, price paid, and where purchase made.
3. Always obtain a receipt, and keep it safely, where you know you can find it if required.

This information will be vital when making an insurance claim, or if you are required to produce a statement of assets.

Periods & Styles

Dates	British Monarch	U.K. Period	French Period
1558-1603	Elizabeth I	Elizabethan	Renaissance
1603-1625	James I	Jacobean	
1625-1649	Charles I	Carolean	Louis XIII (1610-1643)
1649-1660	Commonwealth	Cromwellian	Louis XIV (1643-1715)
1660-1685	Charles II	Restoration	
1685-1689	James II	Restoration	
1689-1694	William & Mary	William & Mary	
1694-1702	William III	William III	
1702-1714	Anne	Queen Anne	
1714-1727	George I	Early Georgian	Régence (1715-1723)
1727-1760	George II	Early Georgian	Louis XV (1723-1774)
1760-1811	George III	Late Georgian	Louis XVI (1774-1793) Directoire (1793-1799) Empire (1799-1815)
1812-1820	George III	Regency	Restauration (1815-1830)
1820-1830	George IV	Regency	
1830-1837	William IV	William IV	Louis Phillipe (1830-1848)
1837-1901	Victoria	Victorian	2nd Empire (1848-1870)
1901-1910	Edward VII	Edwardian	3rd Republic (1871-1940)

Periods & Styles

German Period	U.S. Period	Style	Woods
Renaissance (to c1650)		Gothic	Oak Period (to c1670)
	Early Colonial	Baroque (c1620-1700)	
Renaissance/ Baroque (c1650-1700)			Walnut Period (c1670-1735)
	William & Mary	Rococo (c1695-1760)	
	Dutch Colonial		
Baroque (c1700-1730)	Queen Anne		
	Chippendale (from 1750)		Early Mahogany Period (c1735-1770)
Rococo (c1730-1760)			
Neoclassicism (c1760-1800)	Early Federal (1790-1810)	Neoclassical (c1755-1805)	Late Mahogany Period (c1770-1810)
Empire (c1800-1815)	American Directoire (1798-1804) American Empire (1804-1815)	Empire (c1799-1815)	Exotic Timbers, Calamander, Amboyna, Ebony (c1800-1830)
Biedermeier (c1815-1848)	Later Federal (1810-1830)	Regency (c1812-1830)	
Revivale (c1830-1880)		Eclectic (c1830-1880)	
Jugendstil (c1880-1920)	Victorian	Arts & Crafts (1880-1900)	
		Art Nouveau (c1900-1920)	

18th Century

A Louis XVI clock with ormolu and porcelain mounts.

disorder of the natural world. With a wide range of bright *petit feu* enamel colours now available, European porcelain began to depict realistic representations of flowers and foliage. Blemishes and firing flaws were often covered with sprigs of flowers.

Forms were embellished with delicate repeating rock and shell patterns (the term Rococo being derived from *rocaille* meaning rockwork) and scrolls. The S-scroll

The opening decades of the 18thC saw the development of the Baroque style, which had dominated the previous century. Though elaborately decorated and theatrical, it placed emphasis on order and proportion and was much favoured by monarchs seeking to build capital cities that glorified their rule.

By the 1730s, a relative peace had settled, and European tastes began to turn towards the lighter, more colourful Rococo style. This style, which began in France before moving to Germany, Austria and the rest of Europe, respected and imitated nature. The heavy, formal symmetry of the Baroque was discarded in favour of asymmetry, which allowed a more realistic representation of the

A Philadelphia William & Mary dressing table. c1720

derived from the Classical volute was particularly characteristic of the period, as

A mid-18thC walnut and marquetry marble top commode.

18th Century

A pair of George II fluted sauceboats. 1756

were cartouches made up of multiple S and C scrolls. Furniture carved in this style was frequently smothered with gesso and gilding to create lavish works of art.

The Rococo period was also strongly influenced by the Orient. Chinoiserie, a European interpretation of Chinese decoration, was used on ceramics and furniture. Fantastic beasts, particularly oriental dragons, were used frequently in decoration.

A Chelsea fable candlestick, 'The Fox and the Goat'. c1770

The practise of japanning furniture (applying a shellac varnish to the surface to imitate Japanese lacquer) became common.

After the middle of the century there was another shift in style, this time prompted by the excavations of Herculaneum (in 1738) and Pompeii (in 1748). Robert Adam who embarked on the

A Philadelphia Chippendale walnut side chair. c1750

Grand Tour of Europe from 1754-1758 was among the first to introduce the Neo-classical style in his designs. The trend soon spread.

An American Chippendale walnut tallboy. c1780

INTRODUCTION

Early 19th Century

The Neo-classical style, which began in the late 18thC, dominated the first half of the 19thC.

The Classical urn shape

A Derby bourdalou, with sprigged decoration. c1800

A Neo-classical cast iron urn, with flame finial. c1780

became ubiquitous in all the decorative arts, carved as a finial atop longcase clocks, inlaid as an oval panel on a secretaire à abattant, and, of course, as vases. Swags, lions heads and the Greek key pattern were similarly common across different forms.

Silverware became more formal and less ornate, whilst furniture gave way to straight lines and geometric motifs. Chairs were modelled on the curule (chair sat on by Roman officials) and beds on the triclinium (reclining couch).

Despite a tendency to copy, the Neo-classical designers sought chiefly to create a timeless authentic style using Classical rules of proportion and composition. The increased availability of richly coloured exotic woods and the perfected parquetry and marquetry techniques encouraged cabinet-makers to create complex designs on

An early 19thC giltwood convex mirror, with eagle.

commodes. One of the most popular of these designs was the arabesque: a linear, inter-laced pattern based on foliage and tendrils.

Advancements in glass-ware meant that a wide range of new colours and cut-glass treatments

A Regency window seat, sabre legs and S-scroll arms. c1815

Early 19th Century

A Federal mahogany inlaid sideboard. c1800

crowned himself Emperor of France in 1804. Under his direction, and that of his architects Percier and Fontaine, the French Empire style emerged. Rectilinear forms were even more exaggerated with large pediments or deep plinths, and decorated with military motifs,

(including fluting, diamond cutting, and hobnail) were adopted. The ceramics industry also progressed, for example William Billingsley, who worked at Derby, developed a way of making flowers on porcelain look particularly life-like, by wiping some pigment away for highlights.

While conforming to the same principals, the Neo-classical style varied from country to country. Napoleon Bonaparte

A French Empire lyre-form gilt bronze and marble clock.

such as laurel wreaths, medallions and eagles. Egyptian motifs, inspired by artefacts brought back from Napoleon's recent conquest of Egypt, also featured heavily in the Empire style.

In Britain, the Neo-classical style developed into the Regency style. In Germany it became the relaxed Biedermeir style, in the US: the Federal style, and, in Scandinavia: the light Gustavian style.

A French Empire mahogany oval jardiniere.

A pair of American Empire giltwood X-frame stools.

Late 19th Century

A 19thC German Baroque Revival carved walnut cabinet.

The increasing importance of nationalism, punctuated by the unification of Italy in 1861 and Germany in 1871, led to a revival of earlier styles in the late 19thC. Aided by new innovations in manufacturing techniques, 19thC craftsmen were able to produce a wide variety of pieces that either directly replicated extant pieces or combined details from several earlier styles, sometimes at the expense of decorative cohesion.

The main revivalist style was the Neo-Gothic, though in Britain and Germany it was more of a continuation than a revival. Furniture designers looked to architecture for inspiration, employing pointed arches, latticework, quatrefoils and heraldic motifs in dark heavy woods such as oak. Gothic motifs were applied to ceramics, textiles and silverware. Stained glass was revived and used in domestic architecture.

A French Louis XV Revival giltmetal clock. c1880

Other designers in France and Italy sought inspiration from the Renaissance. Oak and walnut furniture was deeply carved with rows of spindles, strapwork, moulded cornices, and arched doors. Meissen and Sèvres produced grey and white porcelain decorated with Classical figures, grotesques and swags.

A mid-19thC carved walnut and upholstered settee and chair.

A pair of late 19thC armchairs, with mihrab-arched backs.

The Baroque style was revived, though pieces tended to be larger and the style more exaggerated than in the 17thC. Rococo also enjoyed a revival: new technologies allowing more economic reproductions of its intricate foliate designs.

Nationalism also provoked a renewed interest

An L. & J.G. Stickley US Arts & Crafts rocking chair.

in folk motifs and crafts and these were appropriated by industrial manufacturers.

The Arts & Crafts movement, which began c1880, was a rejection of mass-production. Led by writer and art critic, John Ruskin, and designer, William Morris, the movement sought to revive

the skills of medieval craftsmen. Traditional methods were used to produce simple, functional pieces with sparse ornament that showed off the natural beauty of the materials. Ornament included Celtic motifs, enamelling, some

A Rookwood Limoges-style vase. 1922

exotic inlays in furniture, and an explosion of innovative glazes in the ceramics industry. Needlework and weaving were also revived.

With its rejection of machinery, the Arts & Crafts movement was never financially viable in Europe. It only reached its full potential in America, where, with the aid of mass-production, it reached a far wider audience and continued into the 20thC.

A Liberty & Co pewter biscuit box, by Archibald Knox.

Early 20th Century

A Quezal lily lamp, with gold iridescent shades. c1920

The early 20thC was dominated by two contrasting styles.

Art Nouveau began in France and Belgium at the end of the 19thC, its name derived from the Maison de l'Art Nouveau gallery, which was opened by Samuel Bing in Paris in 1895. Like the Rococo style of the 18thC, Art Nouveau was characterised by its pervasive interest in nature, its rich colours, exotic materials and flowing asymmetrical lines. Art Nouveau was the first style to consciously attempt to transform visual culture according to modernist principals.

Designs were elegant and feminine in character, inspired by and decorated with plants, animals and sensuous women with long flowing hair and billowing robes. The *femme-fleur*, half woman and half flower, was a popular motif on furniture, metalware, posters, and ceramics. The whiplash motif, based on swirling plant roots, also became iconic, appearing on many different forms.

Glass makers like Emile Gallé, experimented with cameo glass and iridescent

An Art Nouveau mantel clock, with the figure of a young girl.

glass. Furniture makers used exotic woods with carvings and veneers, whilst metalware was often enamelled and adorned with semi-precious stones.

By 1910, Art Nouveau was becoming increasingly less commercially viable. It had almost disappeared by the onset of World War I.

An Emile Gallé Art Nouveau mahogany display cabinet.

Early 20th Century

Dancer of Kapurthala figure by Demêtre Chiparus. c1925

The innovative style that dominated international design in between the two World Wars was later called Art Deco after the 'Exposition International des Arts Décoratifs et Industriels

A Clarice Cliff 'Bizarre' charger, in the 'Sungold' pattern. 1934

Modernes' held in Paris in 1925. It often featured strong geometric lines and stylized decoration in an eclectic range of materials, from rare ebony to new, inexpensive plastics. It was an age of social and economic advantage. Women were more liberated and therefore appear more animated in Art Deco designs than they did in their Art Nouveau counterparts.

Art Deco was inspired by a multitude of different styles including several historic European styles, Egyptian motifs, contemporary avant-garde art and the urban imagery of the

A Roseville Futura pink and green rectangular vase. c1928

machine age. Furniture, for example, could be lavishly carved and inlaid, or angular, sleek and streamlined like Paul Frankl's 'Skyscraper' range.

Art Deco's influence was immense and it affected the design of skyscrapers, cinemas, trains and cars.

An Art Deco walnut veneered display cabinet, with glazed doors.

Late 20th Century

Levels of supply and demand were seriously depleted after WWII and, in some cases, recovery only happened well into the 1950s. Once economies began to prosper new designers emerged, who were excited by the possibilities of mass production and the new materials available.

A 'Heart' chair by Verner Panton. Designed 1959.

An Aureliano Toso 'Oriente' vase. c1952

For example, Charles Eames had developed a way of moulding plywood in two directions in 1942, and, after the war, he and his wife Ray adapted this technique to produce simple, striking furniture. Other materials used in modernist furniture

included aluminium, stainless steel, glass, and spray-on plastic polymer.

Designs were created with clean line and exuberant colours, many inspired by popular culture, and scientific advances like the moon landing.

Modernist styles varied. One important style was the 'organic modernism' developed in Scandinavia by designers such as Alvar Aalto and Bruno Mathsson. This was inspired by nature, and took a gentler more ergonomic approach using wood rather than plastic or steel.

A Marcel Breuer plywood chaise longue. Late 1950s

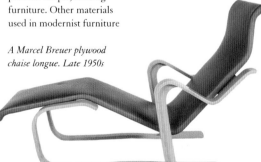

Late 20th Century

An Eero Aarnio Asko pony chair. Designed 1970.

With the end of the 1960s, the modernist Utopian dream gave way to the reality of high-inflation and unemployment. Modernism had almost disappeared by the time the economy recovered in the 1980s. It was replaced with postmodernism. In reaction to the plain decoration and strict forms of mid-century design, Postmodernism experi-

A Ron Arad/One Off Pair of Rover chairs. c1980

mented with witty, irreverent, colourful work and plundered the styles of other centuries. Designers avoided symmetry and often combined bright or clashing colours that challenged the accepted norms of design.

By the early 1990s, this mix of styles was losing favour and was replaced by simpler designs in glass, brushed metals, single coloured plastic and untreated wood, where the medium accentuated the form of the work.

The digital revolution that followed inspired smooth and technical designs. The internet enabled designers to share ideas and images at speed

An Albert Paley forged milled steel fireplace surround. 1980s

and helped create an international culture. This allowed postmodernism to become a truly global style.

A Tahiti table lamp, by Ettore Sottsass for Memphis. 1981

Design Registration Marks

One of the most useful marks for dating is the Design Registration mark. Registration began in 1839 following the Copyright of Design Act. The insignia (diamond-shaped mark) was used from 1842. The insignia also showed what material the item was made from (its class) and how many items were included (bundle or package). The Rd in the centre of the diamond stands for registered design.

THE DESIGN REGISTRATION MARK

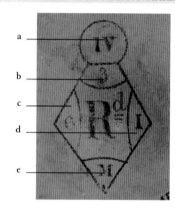

1842-67
a = class
b = year
c = month
d = day
e = bundle

1868-83
a = class
b = day
c = bundle
d = year
e = month

YEAR
The letters were not used in sequence but as follows:
1842-1867 (features a number in the right hand corner of the diamond)

A – 1845	G – 1863	M – 1859	S – 1849	Y – 1853
B – 1858	H – 1843	N – 1864	T – 1867	Z – 1860
C – 1844	I – 1846	O – 1862	U – 1848	
D – 1852	J – 1854	P – 1851	V – 1850	
E – 1855	K – 1857	Q – 1866	W – 1865	
F – 1847	L – 1856	R – 1861	X – 1842	

1868-1883 (letter in the right hand corner of the diamond)

A – 1871	F – 1873	K – 1883	U – 1874
C – 1870	H – 1869	L – 1882	V – 1876
D – 1878	I – 1872	P – 1877	X – 1868
E – 1881	J – 1880	S – 1875	Y – 1879

The exceptions to these are: in 1857 the letter R was used from 1-19 September. In 1860 the letter K was used for December. From 1-6 March 1878, W was used for the year in place of D, and G was used for the month in place of W.

THE DESIGN REGISTRATION MARK - continued

MONTHS
The months from both periods are shown as follows:

A – December	E – May	K – November
B – October	G – February	M – June
C/O – January	H – April	R – August
D – September	I – July	W – March

CLASS
Sometimes the clerks mis-classified items so it is possible to find a bookbinding misfiled as a carpet.

Class 1 - Metal
Class 2 - Wood
Class 3 - Glass
Class 4 - Earthenware
Class 5 - Paper Hangings
Class 6 - Carpets
Class 7 - Printed Shawls
Class 8 - Other Shawls
Class 9 - Yarn
Class 10 - Printed Fabrics
Class 11 - Furnitures (printed fabrics)
Class 12 (i) - Other Fabrics
Class 12 (ii) - Other Fabrics (Damasks)
Class 13 - Lace

REGISTERED NUMBER
A series of consecutive numbers were used from 1884, nearly always prefixed by Rd or Rd No (Registered or Registered Number). This guide is an estimate only:

1: 1884	291241: 1897	673,750: 1920
19754: 1885	311658: 1898	751,160: 1930
40480: 1886	331707: 1899	837,520: 1940
64520: 1887	351202: 1900	860,854: 1950
90483: 1888	368154: 1901	895,000: 1960
116648: 1889	385500: 1902	944,932: 1970
141273: 1890	402500: 1903	993,012: 1980
163767: 1891	420000: 1904	2,007,720: 1990
185713: 1892	447000: 1905	2,089,190: 2000
205240: 1893	471000: 1906	
224720: 1894	494000: 1907	
246975: 1895	519000: 1908	*The system is still*
268393: 1896	550000: 1909	*in use today*

INTRODUCTION

Ceramic year cyphers

PATTERN NUMBERS

Pattern numbers can indicate a particular porcelain factory although few are unique to one factory. Examples are:

Chamberlain-Worcester

Pattern nos started c1790. Reached

    100 by 1797
    400 by 1807
    610 by 1812
    790 by 1817
    1000 by 1822

numbers then go to   1752

    2000 – 2624
    3000 – 3099
    1000 – 4099
    5000 – 5019

Coalport: John Rose & Co

Pattern nos. started c1805. 1-999 used to c1825.

2/1; 2/2 – 2/999 to c1832
3/1; 3/2 – 3/999 used c1832-38
4/1; 4/2 – 4/1000 used c1838-43
5/1; 5/2 – 5/1000 used c1843-50

ROOKWOOD

The Rookwood mark is very prescriptive. The flame mark with Rookwood monogram was used from 1886 with an extra flame used each year – by 1900 there were 14 flames. In 1901 the Roman Numeral 1 was added below and changed accordingly with each year.

Ceramic year cyphers

WEDGWOOD

Wedgwood used an impressed mark from c1759 onwards. From 1891 "ENGLAND" was added.

Impressed year letters: where there is a group of three letters, the third denotes year.

O — 1860	Y — 1870	I — 1880
P — 1861	Z — 1871	J — 1881
Q — 1862	A — 1872	K — 1882
R — 1863	B — 1873	L — 1883
S — 1864	C — 1874	M — 1884
T — 1865	D — 1875	N — 1885
U — 1866	E — 1876	O — 1886
V — 1867	F — 1877	P — 1887
W — 1868	G — 1878	Q — 1888
X — 1869	H — 1879	R — 1889
		S — 1890
		T — 1891
		U — 1892
		V — 1893
		M — 1894
		X — 1895
		Y — 1896
		Z — 1897

ROYAL WORCESTER

In 1862 new date codes were used at Royal Worcester. A series of number and letter codes were used until 1891 when the Royal Worcester England mark was first used. In 1892 a system of dots were added to the mark, with a dot added for each year from 1892. Here there are 15 dots: six either side of the crown and three beneath it showing this piece was made in 1906.

Understanding other marks

COUNTRY NAME

In 1890 the American Congress passed legislation which meant a tariff had to be paid on all imports of china, glass, leather and metal. As a result, from 1891, all goods which might be imported to America were marked with the country of origin such as "France" or "England".

MADE IN...

A Royal coat of arms in a mark shows the item was made no earlier than 1800 but could be much later. From 1914 wares were often marked "Made in ..." and the country of origin. From 1912 "Made in ..." and the country of origin had to be in English.

BONE CHINA

"Bone China" and "English bone China" are 20thC marks. The word "Royal" in a British firm's name tends to date from the late 19thC or 20thC rather than any earlier.

US PATENTS

American designs may be registered by patent number, design number and/or trademark. The first patent number was issued in 1836. The number recorded on an article shows the date it was registered not necessarily the date it was made. The design patent and number protect the

shape, colour or pattern of an item. The first number was issued in 1843. Trademarks – usually denoted by the symbol ^{TM} – have been used since 1870 and are applied to names, phrases and logos.

Understanding other marks

MADE IN OCCUPIED JAPAN

From the end of WWII in 1945 and until 1952, items imported from Japan to the US had to be marked to indicate that they came from Occupied Japan. Pieces marked "Occupied Japan" and "Made in Occupied Japan" were made during this time.

MADE IN USSR

From c1925 until 1991 items made in the Union of Soviet Socialist Republics (or Soviet Union) were marked "Made in USSR". Since 1991 the names of the individual countries have been used: Russia, Estonia, Latvia, Lithuania, Belarus, Ukraine, Moldova and Georgia etc.

MADE IN GERMAN ZONE

From the end of WWII in 1945 and until 1949, items made in the US, British, French and Soviet occupied zones of Germany were marked as such. The marks Federal Republic of Germany (West Germany) or German Democratic Republic (West Germany) date from 1949-1990.

OTHER MARKS...

Pattern numbers don't denote a specific factory but tend to date from after 1815 and are USUALLY much later.

"Limited" or "Ltd." tends to denote a date after 1861 – but became much more common after 1885.

In the UK an impressed "Trade Mark" can be assumed to be after 1862. In the US after 1876.

Items marked "copyright" date from after 1858 but are usually 20thC. The © mark was introduced in 1914.

The French word for patented – "déposé" – and the German phrase – "Gesetzlich Geschützt (Ges. Gesch)" – were first used c1900.

Introduction

CERAMICS

The Crucial Questions

The Chinese discovered the art of making porcelain in the Tang Dynasty (618–906AD). By the end of the 17thC it had become a European obsession to uncover the secret, since Chinese porcelain was being exported to Europe in ever increasing quantities. Johann Böttger at Meissen discovered the formula for hard paste porcelain in the early years of the 18thC. By 1770 the secret had spread to Vienna, Strasbourg, Frankenthal and Nymphenburg. In France, Vincennes and Sèvres first produced soft paste porcelain in 1745–72. Soft paste porcelain was produced at most of the 18thC English and Welsh factories. Only Plymouth, Bristol and Newhall used hard paste.

There are three essential questions

1. The distinction between pottery and porcelain.
2. The distinction between hard and soft paste porcelain.
3. The distinction between hand-painted and printed wares.

1. The earthenware body of 18thC **pottery** was often coarse and heavy in comparison with the delicate translucency of Chinese porcelain. At the end of the 17thC, the Staffordshire potteries discovered that salt added to the glaze led to a near white salt-glazed stoneware.

The production of **porcelain** relied on the discovery of china clay and china stone. In 1745, William Cookworthy from Plymouth discovered china clay and china stone (petuntse) in England. This was the beginning of English hard paste porcelain. Soon Lund's factory at Bristol and those at Bow and Chelsea were making soft paste porcelain using frit or soapstone in place of china stone.

Now the distinction: **pottery** includes anything made from baked clay. It includes a number of different materials: with earthenwares and stonewares covered in many glazes. **Porcelain** is a hard, translucent white substance made from china clay and china stone; it has a clear ringing sound when struck. The most common distinction between pottery and porcelain is that pottery is not translucent and porcelain is. While as a simple rule this has some truth, a number of porcelains have little translucency.

2. Porcelain is sub-divided into hard and soft paste. The best way to tell them apart is to study the difference between damaged examples.

- **Hard paste**: fired at a higher temperature than soft paste; cold feel to the touch; chip is flint- or glass-like; hard, glittery glaze fused to the paste; can become translucent during second firing; kaolin content makes it more refined.

- **Soft paste**: a file will cut easily into soft paste; chip is granular; warmer feeling to the touch; less stable in the kiln – figures were difficult to fire (no English soft paste figures compare with those of German factories); glaze was soft as it tended not to fuse into the body as much as glaze on hard paste and was liable to pooling and crazing; early soft paste prone to discoloration.

3. There are four main types of decoration on porcelain: underglaze, overglaze, painted and printed. It is vital to tell the difference between hand-painted and printed decoration. Easy identification comes with constantly comparing pieces. These points may help:

- A **hand-painted** pattern is achieved by brush strokes and has a fluidity that is impossible with a print.

- Brush work is most obvious where there is shading of colour.
- The brush tends to be less precise than an engraving – note the hatch marks evident on a print.
- A **printed** pattern results from an etched or engraved copper plate.
- Most underglaze work was effected in blue which appeared black when applied, as the true colour only appeared after firing.
- Overglaze printing was introduced in the mid-1750s, at least five years before underglaze.

Berlin

CERAMICS

BERLIN

In 1763, Frederick the Great bought a bankrupt pottery factory, renamed it the Royal Porcelain Factory.

- Late 18thC: Rococo-style wares, with trelliswork, flowers and pierced rims; Neo-classical wares.
- First half 19thC: "cabinet" cups and tea services.
- c1830: vases based on urns with

Classical motifs. High-quality decorated porcelain, particularly plaques, made to the early 20thC.

BOCH FRÈRES

In 1841, the Keramis Pottery was established at La Louvière, Belgium, by the Boch Family. Boch Frères Art Deco pottery made in 1920s and 30s.

- Design and decoration overseen by Charles Catteau from 1906-45.
- Catteau's wares mostly in vibrant cloisonné enamels, typically

azure-blue and yellow, on craquelure ground. Hand decoration typical, often with symmetrical or frieze patterns. Pottery active until WW2.

BOW

Founded in mid-18thC at Stratford Langthorne, Essex. One of the first two porcelain factories in England.

- Blue and white wares: Early period 1749–54: thickly potted, glaze often blue/green. Middle period 1755–65: darker blue, thinly potted. Relatively heavy. Late period 1765–76: marked deterioration in quality.
- Early polychrome wares: decorated in 'famille rose' colours.
- In 1775, factory acquired by W. Duesbury. All Bow moulds and tools moved to Derby porcelain factory.

BRISTOL DELFT

A number of potteries in Bristol produced tin-glazed earthenware in the late 17thC/18thC.

- Late 17thC: blue-dash chargers, splashily painted in maiolica colours with portraits/flowers.
- From c1720: chinoiseries in blue and white; plates, punch-bowls, etc.
- After c1755: bianco sopra bianco technique sometimes adopted for borders of plates.
- From c1784: production of tin-glazed wares gave way to cream-coloured earthenware, which was made until 1884.

BRISTOL PORCELAIN

The first porcelain factory at Bristol was founded in 1749. Its moulds were sold to Worcester in 1752. William Cookworthy transferred his Plymouth factory to Bristol in 1770.

- Early wares difficult to differentiate from Plymouth, same firing imperfections like smoky ivory glaze and wreathing in the body. The body can have tears/firing cracks.

- Champion took over in 1773.
- Mid-late 1770s wares are typically Neo-classical in style, decorated with swags and scattered flowers.
- Later Bristol colours are sharp. Gilding quality excellent.
- Factory closed in 1781.

CAUGHLEY

A pottery established at Caughley, Shropshire, soon after 1750. It began producing porcelain after it was taken over by Thomas Turner in 1772. In 1775, Robert Hancock, formerly of Worcester, joined the factory and introduced transfer printing in blue underglaze.

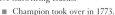

- Painted wares tend to be earlier than printed ones.

- From 1780s: many pieces heightened in gilding.
- Often confused with Worcester as they have many patterns in common, eg "Fence".
- Soapstone type-body often shows orange to transmitted light. 1799: works sold to Coalport.

Chantilly

CHANTILLY

Founded 1725, only soft paste porcelain made, covered until c1735 (and sometimes later) with an opaque tin glaze.

- High quality white finish.
- Mid 18thC: European floral styles.
- 1750s: transparent lead glaze. Tends to copy Meissen and Vincennes.
- From 1755–1780: floral designs produced, often in one colour.
- Basically ceased by end 18thC.

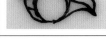

CHELSEA

The factory's early history is very vague but it may have acquired the knowledge of porcelain manufacture in 1742.

Triangle Period 1745–49

- Wares scarce and costly.
- Mainly undecorated.
- Body comparatively thick, slightly chalky with "glassy" glaze.

Raised Anchor Period 1749–52

- Paste now improved.
- Mostly restrained decoration, either Kakiemon or sparse floral work.
- Most collectable wares of this and the Red Anchor period was fable decorated.
- Creamy, waxy appearance of glaze virtually indistinguishable from Red Anchor glaze.

Red Anchor Period 1752–56 (see mark below)

- Significant Meissen influence.
- Glaze now slightly opaque. Paste smoother.
- Figures unsurpassed by any other English factory.
- Chelsea "toys" are rare and expensive.

Gold Anchor Period 1757–69

- Rococo influence, rich gilding and characteristic mazarine blue.
- Decoration quite florid style, especially in comparison to earlier painting.
- Influenced by Sèvres.
- Thick glaze can craze.

CLIFF, CLARICE (1899-1972)

Clarice Cliff began work as a lithographer at Wilkinson's Royal Staffordshire Pottery in 1916. She was given her own studio at Newport Pottery in 1925 where she conceived or oversaw more than 500 shapes and 2,000 patterns until 1940.

■ Popular 'Bizarre' range from 1928 until 1935, characterised by hand-applied, brightly coloured patterns in a characteristically Art Deco style.

■ Bizarre range noted for innovative forms including honeycomb teapot, concial sugar shakers and inverted conical bowl.

■ Later patterns developed towards a more elaborate, abstract and bold style, particularly in the 'Fantasque' range.

■ Early Clarice Cliff is rare and can be distinguished by thickly applied paint with visible brush strokes and black outlines.

■ Clarice Cliff figures are extremely rare and valuable.

COALPORT

Founded in early 1790s at Coalbrookdale. Still active.

■ Early blue and white wares like Caughley.

■ 1820: leadless glaze invented followed by best period: white, hard feldspar porcelain, highly translucent. Rococo wares of late 1820s-30s often confused with Rockingham.

DAVENPORT

Factory making earthenware started by John Davenport at Longport, Staffordshire, in 1793, porcelain production followed from 1820.

■ Pieces marked "Longport" rare.

■ Named flowers on botanical wares can add 50% to value.

■ The factory closed in 1887.

CERAMICS

DERBY

In 1756, William Duesbury, John Heath and André Planché started what became the first Derby Porcelain Factory.

Early period 1756-69

- Restrained decoration, with much of the body left plain, in the Meissen style.
- Excellent body, sometimes with faintly bluish appearance.
- In 1770, Duesbury bought the Chelsea factory and ran it until 1784 in conjunction with Derby.

Chelsea-Derby 1770-84

- Chelsea-Derby figures made at Derby.
- Unglazed white biscuit Derby figures. Move away from the academic Meissen style towards the more fashionable French taste.
- 1770s: body frequently of silky appearance and bluish-white tone.
- 1780s: body very smooth, white glaze. Painting on such pieces is superb, especially landscapes of Jockey Hill and Zachariah Boreman.
- 1780s and 1790s: noted for exceptional botanical painting by "Quaker" Pegg and John Brewer.
- Around 1800 the body degenerated, was somewhat thicker, and the glaze tended to crackle and allow discolouration.
- Products made at both factories bore the same mark – an anchor and the letter D.

Crown Derby 1784-1811

- Factory adopted a crowned D as its mark.
- Many earlier styles continued to be made. Other products included simply decorated table-wares, Neo-classical in shape and sometimes painted with fresh naturalistic flowers, by William Billingsley and others. Notable statuettes were produced after models by Jean-Jacques Spängler and Pierre Stephan.

Bloor Derby 1811-45

- Period of steady decline in which the factory lost all individuality.

Royal Crown Derby

- Established in 1876.
- Factory still active.

ROYAL DOULTON

Doulton & Co. established by John Doulton at Lambeth, South London, in 1815, as 'Doulton & Watts' and was known as such until 1851.

- Initially specialized in useful stoneware.
- c1860: revival of earlier types of stoneware, notably copies of 18thC stoneware vessels, and salt-glazed wares with blue decoration.
- c1870: Doulton began producing art pottery. Hand-thrown, glazed in subdued brown, blue and grey by students of Lambeth School of Art, including George Tinworth, and Hannah, Florence and Arthur Barlow.
- 1883: bought major shareholding in Pinder, Bourne & Co. in Burslem, Staffordshire. The factory produced tableware as well as ornaments and earthenwares.
- 1902: became Royal Doulton.
- 1920-30: produced Art Deco functional tablewares/decorative pieces; and collectable bone china figures.
- 1956: Lambeth factory closed.
- 2005: Burslem factory closed.

DRESDEN

In the late 19thC/early 20thC there were at least 40 porcelain workshops or decorators in and around the Saxon capital of Dresden, most of them copying the Meissen style.

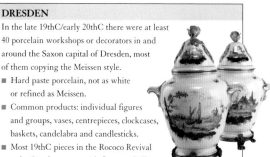

- Hard paste porcelain, not as white or refined as Meissen.
- Common products: individual figures and groups, vases, centrepieces, clockcases, baskets, candelabra and candlesticks.
- Most 19thC pieces in the Rococo Revival style. Overly ornate, with flowers, shells, scrollwork and figures all together, painted in garish tones.
- A distinctive feature is intricate lacework made by dipping real lace into liquid paste and firing it.
- Notable factories: Carl Thieme in Potschappel.

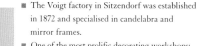

- The Voigt factory in Sitzendorf was established in 1872 and specialised in candelabra and mirror frames.
- One of the most prolific decorating workshops: Helena Wolfson est. 1843 in Dresden.

Fulper

FULPER

Samuel Hill opened a pottery in c1815 at Flemington, New Jersey.

- 19thC: produced only utilitarian wares. Called Fulper from 1899.
- 1909: art pottery made by William H Fulper II.
- Simple shapes decorated with crystalline glaze, under the name "Vasekraft".

- J. Martin Stangl joins the company in 1910 and goes on to buy it in 1930. Renamed Stangl Pottery in 1955.

GOLDSCHEIDER

Goldscheider Manufactory & Majolica Factory founded in Vienna in 1885, by Friederich Goldscheider.

- Mostly unglazed red earthenware cold painted to simulate Vienna bronzes.
- Elaborate moulds used for early wares and into Art Deco period, allowed meticulous detail.
- Art Deco figures mostly produced 1922-35.

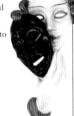

    Emphasis on copying current fashions. Best figures by leading sculptors, including Josef Lorenzl and Stefan Dakon.
- Factory closed in 1953.

GRUEBY

The Grueby Faience Co. was established in 1894 in Boston, Massachusetts, and was originally dedicated to manufacturing architectural bricks and tiles. Art ware manufacture began in 1897.

- Hard earthenware vessels, covered with matt glazes in a range of green hues, like moss green, and brown and ochre.
- Patterns inspired by nature/the organic shapes seen in the work of Auguste Delaherche.
- Collection of lamps produced in collaboration with Tiffany.
- Art ware usually marked "Grueby" alongside vegetal motif.

LIVERPOOL

In the 1750s, a number of porcelain-factories operated in close proximity to one another in Liverpool.

Richard Chaffers & Partners c1754–65

- In 1755, Chaffers engaged Robert Podmore as manager in return for the secret "of making earthenware in imitation of or to resemble china ware".
- Early phosphatic wares have a greyish body, while later wares are noticeably whiter.

Philip Christian c1765–76

- Philip Christian took over Richard Chaffer's factory upon his death.
- In 1772, Christian renewed his licence to mine steatite at Predannak, Cornwall.
- In 1776, Philip Christian and Son sold their interest and ceased manufacturing.

James, John and Seth Pennington c1769–99

- Majority blue and white.

- Some highly collectable ship painted dated jugs and bowls produced 1770s/80s.
- Very dark underglaze blue used. 1770s and '80s. Glaze sometimes tinted.

Samuel Gilbody c1754–61

- Purchased his father's factory from his mother in c1754.
- Rarest of all Liverpool groups.
- A sometimes blurred greyish underglaze blue, may be enamelled in iron red. Typical glaze smooth and silky.

William Reid c1755–61

- Wares mainly blue and white.
- Often a crude and semi-opaque body. Glaze opacified.
- Reid became bankrupt in 1761 and factory occupied by William Ball.

William Ball c1755–69

- Large variety of shapes. Elaborate Rococo sauceboats were a speciality.
- Decoration often resembled delftware.

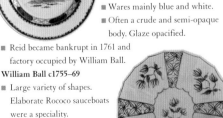

CERAMICS

HÖCHST

In 1746, Adam Friedrich von Löwenfink founded a faience factory in Höchst, near Mainz. The factory began producing porcelain in 1750 after the arrival of arcanist Josef Jakob Ringler.

■ Porcelain figures modelled by craftsmen including Simon Feilner, Johan Friedrich Lück, Karl Gottlob Lück, and Johann Peter Melchior, who became master modeller in 1767.

■ Other wares were painted with landscape vignettes featuring figures.

■ Factory closed in 1796. Melchior moulds sold to Damm Pottery.

LONGTON HALL

Founded in 1749 by William Jenkinson, the Longton Hall porcelain factory was the first porcelain factory in Staffordshire.

■ Run by William Littler and William Nicklin.
■ Early period: pieces often thickly potted. Porcelain: glassy soft-paste type. Glaze can have a greenish-grey appearance.
■ c1754-57: best quality porcelain, ideal for making forms of fruit, vegetables and leaves that dominated wares.
■ Important painters: "Castle painter" and the "trembly rose" painter. All wares are now rare.
■ Factory closed in 1760.

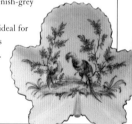

LOWESTOFT

The Lowestoft porcelain factory was founded in 1757 and produced soft paste porcelain using bone ash, similar to Bow.

■ Specialized in simple form tablewares decorated in underglaze blue (painted or transfer-printed), generally with chinoiseries.
■ Collectors interested in unusual shapes.

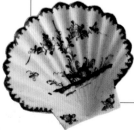

■ Damage tends to stain brown.
■ Many pieces pre-1775 numbered inside footrim or on base.
■ Factory closed c1800, but manager, Robert Allen, continued to work as a porcelain painter, using a muffle kiln.

Martin Brothers

LUNEVILLE

In 1731, Jacques Chambrette founded a faience factory in Lunéville. It produced bold Rococo tablewares in strong colours.

■ Noteable for figures: large faience lions and dogs, and small figures in *terre de pipe* after models by Paul Louis Cyfflé: employed c1752-66.

■ Chambrette died in 1758, leaving the factory to his son and son-in-law.
■ Factory renamed Manufacture Royal. Production of English-style cream-coloured earthenware began.
■ Factory sold in 1788 to Sebastian Keller and partner, whose descendants ran it throughout the 19thC.

MARSEILLE

During the 18thC and early 19thC there were twelve faience factories in Marseilles.

■ Looser and more spontaneous design than on wares produced in northern France.

■ Early 18thC: bold chinoiseries in high-fired (*grand-feu*) colours popular.
■ From c1750, focused on low-fired (*petit-feu*) enamelled decoration. Forms diverse and lively, in keeping with the Rococo style.
■ Late 18thC: competition from porcelain/English creamware forced most factories to close.

MARTIN BROTHERS

In 1873, established a studio pottery in Fulham, London. Led by Robert Wallace Martin, who studied at the Lambeth School of Art, produced a range of fanciful salt-glazed stoneware.
Joined by brothers Charles, Walter and Edwin.

■ Figures of animals, most famously birds, with human features, vases, tobacco jars.

■ Used a muted palette.
■ Early pieces signed "Martin". Pieces made 1882-1914 usually incised "RW Martin & Brothers London & Southall". Closed in 1914.

Meissen

CERAMICS

MEISSEN

The first porcelain factory in Europe,
founded in Germany in 1710. Great period
began in 1720 with the appointment of
J. G. Höroldt as chief painter.

- First wares: director, J. F. Böttger's fine,
  extremely hard red stoneware, with
  engraved designs and lacquer painting.
  Stoneware superseded by white hard paste, discovered
  by Böttger and Tschirnhaus c1709.

- 1720–50: enamelling on Meissen unsurpassed.
  Löwenfink: bold, flamboyant chinoiserie or Japonnaise
  subjects, often derived from the engravings of
  Petruschenk, particularly on Augustus Rex wares.
  J. G. Höroldt: elaborate miniature chinoiserie
  figure subjects. C. F. Höroldt: European and
  Levantine quay scenes.

- Crossed swords factory mark used from 1723.

- In late 1720s, a glassier, harder looking paste
  introduced.

- Best figures late 1730s and early 1740s, especially
  the great Commedia dell'Arte figures/
  groups. Finest Meissen figures by
  J. J. Kändler (chief modeller from 1733).

- Other distinguished modellers: Paul
  Reinicke and J. F. Eberlein.

- Extensive range of dinner services, tea
  and coffee services, candlesticks, other
  useful/decorative wares. Kändler designed the
  factory's most famous service, known as the 'Swan' service.

- The naturalistic flower subjects of the 1740s gradually became
  less realistic and moved towards the
  manier Blumen of the 1750s/60s.

- 1763: complete reorganisation of
  factory as Rococo out of style.
  Less-ornate Louis XVI style
  tablewares produced.

- Early 19thC: mass production
  of popular styles: Biedermier
  style, early Neo-classical style.

  - Mid-19thC onwards:
    mass production
    of revived Rococo style,
    using 18thC moulds.
  - Factory still active.

MENNECY

Originally founded in 1734 in Paris,
moved to Mennecy in 1748, then to
Bourg-la-Reine in 1773.

- Soft-paste porcelain.
- c1780: factory stopped
  producing porcelain in favour
  of cream-coloured earthenware.
- Factory closed 1806.

MINTON

Founded at Stoke-on-Trent, Staffordshire, in 1793, produced
earthenware. Began to make porcelain c1798.

- 1849: Joseph-François Léon Arnoux becomes artistic director,
  decoration becomes richer. Vibrant ground colours, excellent
  gilding. Particularly successful turquoise ground.
  Famous for majolica.
  - c1873: "Minton"
    mark became
    "Mintons".
  - Factory still open.

MOORCROFT

William Moorcroft (1872-1945) became
director of the Art Pottery at James
Macintyre and Co. in Burselm, in 1898.

- Aurelian Ware: transfer-
  printed with gilding.
- Florian Ware: hand painted,
  brightly coloured Art Nouveau patterns.
- Factory still active.

MORGAN, WILLIAM DE (1839-1917)

Part of the influential circle of artist-
craftsmen led by William Morris.

- Inspired by Hispano-Moresque and
  Persian wares. Flat patterns.
- Rich colours: gold, red,
  purple, green, turquoise.
- 1888: founded pottery at
  Fulham with Hasley
  Ricardo.

CERAMICS

MOUSTIERS

One of the most important and influential groups of French faience factories was located in Moustiers, near Marseilles.

- Most notable factory founded by Antoine Clérissy. Best wares c1710-40: wide variety of objects decorated in soft blue on very smooth, milky white ground, with grotesques and arabesque ornament.
- Painting in high temperature colours introduced to Moustiers by J. Olerys.
- 1770s: the factory of Jean-Bapiste Ferrat began producing wares decorated in enamel colours.
- Faience continues to be made at Moustiers.

NANTGARW

The Nantgarw porcelain factory was founded by William Billingsley in South Wales in 1813.

- Glassy translucent artificial porcelain, thick soft glaze.
- Nantgarw porcelain difficult to control, so wares were mainly plates which were ideal for flower painting.
- Some products were painted at independent decorating studios in London.
- 1820: factory closed due to lack of profit.
- Factory mark: impressed "NANT-GARW" with "C.W." below.
- In 1833, W.H. Pardoe re-opened the factory, which closed again in 1920.

NEW HALL

New Hall porcelain factory established in Staffordshire in 1781 by a group of partners who bought Richard Champion's patent and produced a variation on hard-paste porcelain: 'hybrid hard paste'.

- Factory aimed at mass market. Bulk of wares: tea and coffee services in limited range of patterns.
- Initially wares imitating Chinese export wares: elaborate groups of mandarins in exotic landscapes.
- From 1791, much simpler patterns: isolated sprigs of flowers in famille rose colours.
- Factory closed 1835.

North Dakota School of Mines

NEWCOMB

Pottery founded by Ellsworth Woodwood in 1895 at H. Sophie Newcomb Memorial College, New Orleans, Louisiana.

- Decorators largely students at the college. The intention being that they would learn skills they could bring to the labour force.
- Notable designers and instructors: Sadie Irvine, Harriet Joor, Anna Frances Simpson, and Henrietta Bailey.
- Vases decorated with imagery of indigenous flora and fauna and bayou scenes. Shapes inspired by Oriental and peasant pottery.
- Early wares: palette of yellow, blue, green and black; clear high glaze.
- Post-1910: matt glazes in soft blues, whites, and creams.
- Decline in quality after 1931.
- Work dating c1898-1910 most desirable.

- Mark: firm's symbol, artist's cipher, the potter's mark, designated date.
- 1940: production ceased.

NIDERVILLER

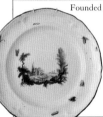

Founded in 1754 in Lorraine, France, made faience.

- 1770-71: sold to Comte de Custine. Faience with *décors bois* and porcelain figures.
- Late 19thC onwards: copies of 18thC wares from original moulds.
- Factory still active.

NORTH DAKOTA SCHOOL OF MINES

Established in 1892 at University of North Dakota. Pieces made by ceramics students.

- Influenced by Arts & Crafts movement, as well as Art Noveau and Art Deco.
- Some feature flora and fauna; Native American/western motifs; farming/hunting scenes. Gradation of colour.
- Early pieces marked "U.N.D.". Most pieces stamped with full name of university. Pottery still active.

Paris

CERAMICS

PARIS

There were faience factories in Paris from the
early 17thC, increasing in number during the
18thC, until there were fourteen in 1789.

■ Most notable faience factories: Digne
factory, and the Louis François Ollivier
factory, which specialized in stove-painted
in enamel.

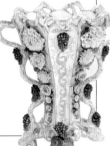

■ Many Paris factories produced porcelain from the
mid-to late 18thC.

■ First quarter 19thC: porcelain factories followed the 18thC
emphasis on the aesthetic.

■ By 1830: many factories were forced to streamline production
and simplify decorative techniques such as printed decoration.

■ Considerable reliance on Rococo/Neo-classical styles, though
some innovation.

La Courtille factory

■ Most productive factory. Founded in 1771 by Jean-Baptiste
Locré de Roissey. First wares Meissen-style; others Louis XVI-
style. Factory closed c1840.

Jacob Petit factory

■ Most prominent porcelain manufacturer in Paris from the
1830s. Initially, produced simple wares with meticulously
modelled or painted flowers.

■ By the mid-1830s, he had mastered the historical revival styles:
mainly Rococo influences, combined with Gothic and
Renaissance revival. Few areas left undecorated.

■ Petit bankrupt in 1848. Factory sold in 1862 to an employee.

Other factories

■ Most other notable Paris factories were under the protection of
members of the royal family/nobility.

■ Factory in the Petite Rue Saint-Giles, founded in 1785 by
François-Maurice Honoré, was under the patronage of the
Duchesse D'Angoulême.

■ Later run in collaboration with other establishments like that of
Pierre-Louis Dagoty, and became the
leading Paris factory by 1807,
supplying the Empress Joséphine
and the Imperial Court.

■ Dagoty factory closed in 1867.

Rhead, Frederick Hurten

PINXTON

Pinxton porcelain factory was established at Pinxton in
Derbyshire, in 1796 by William Billingsley under the patronage
of local landowner, John Coke.

- 1796-1801: translucent soft-paste porcelain containing bone ash,
  painted with flowers in the style of Derby.
- From c1803: under management of John Cutts.
- Wares: rather coarse, nearly opaque porcelain, sometimes
  decorated with landscapes, including named
  local views. May also have decorated
  blanks from other sources.

  - Mark: impressed capital letters
    common on early wares.
  - Factory closed 1813.

PLYMOUTH

The first factory to make hard paste porcelain in England.

- Founded by William Cookworthy in 1768, who discovered
  kaolin/patented the use of this material with petuntse.
- Early wares: thick, bobbly glaze. Mugs and sauceboats
  decorated in underglaze blue. Clumsy figures copied from
  Bow/Longton Hall. Cookworthy returned to Bristol in 1770.
- Quality improved under Richard Champion (director from
  1774), but products still mostly
  unsuccessful imitations of
  Meissen, Sèvres or Derby. Some
  richly decorated vases.

- 1781: Champion sold patent to
  New Hall and the factory closed.

RHEAD, FREDERICK HURTEN (1880-1942)

From family of British potters, including father,
Frederick A; brother, Harry; sister, Charlotte.

- 1902: immigrated to USA.
- 1903-04: Worked for Weller pottery.
- 1904-08: Art director at Roseville. Designed
  'Della Robbia' range.
- Taught at the University City Pottery
  (1910), and Arequipa pottery (1911-18).
- 1913-17: Set up pottery with wife at Santa
  Barbara.
- From 1920: Secretary of the Art Division of
  the American Ceramic Society.

Rookwood

ROOKWOOD

Rookwood Pottery of Cincinnati, Ohio, is acknowledged to be the most important producer of American art pottery, in terms of quality, innovation, longevity, and volume.

- Founded by Maria Longworth Nichols in 1880.
- 1883: William Watts Taylor took charge as manager. Rookwood began to succeed financially as a business.
- Only decorative wares produced. Mainly vases or ornamental jugs of simple, generally oriental shapes.
- 1890: Rookwood Pottery Company was incorporated in Ohio with Taylor as president. Employing over 50 staff artists, Rookwood created lines that would be imitated by companies all over the country:

Standard glaze (1884)
Translucent high gloss that gave all colours a yellow-brown hue.

Iris glaze (1884)
Colourless glaze retaining the richness and depth of the Standard. By 1912, Iris's high lead content recognised as health hazard and production ceased.

Sea Green glaze (c1885)
Used almost exclusively for seascapes and fish, because of its blue-green colour. Largely abandoned by 1904.

Matte glaze (c1900)
Flat and opaque with a coarse texture.

Vellum glaze (1900)
Diffuses the painted decoration (usually plants or landscapes) it covers, giving an Impressionist appearance. Vellum also available with green and yellow tints. Most Vellum ware produced before 1915.

- All pieces marked with initials of the decorator and a symbol indicating the year it was made.

- Pottery survived two World Wars and the Depression, but wares markedly inferior.
- Pottery closed in 1967.

ROCKINGHAM

The Rockingham pottery and porcelain factory was established on the estate of the Marquis of Rockingham in Yorkshire in the 1820s.

- Porcelain manufactured from 1826 when Earl Fitzwilliam (heir to the Rockingham estates) helped finance the factory. The griffin from his family crest adopted as a mark.

  - Porcelain softer than contemporaries. Smoky ivory/oatmeal colour.
  - Glaze had a tendency to irregular fine crazing.
    - Rococo style decoration, frequently excellent quality flower painting.
    - Factory closed in 1847.

ROSENTHAL

The Rosenthal Porcelain Factory was founded in Selb, Bavaria, in 1879, by Philipp Rosenthal.

- 1910: Ornamental porcelain department opened.
- Range of Art Deco figurines designed 1924-39.
- Modellers included Dorothea Charol: exotic dancers in the 1920s, and Clarie Weiss: Art Deco series of Four Seasons in 1931.
- 1925-35: Art Deco tableware produced.

  - All Rosenthal clearly marked with crown and lettering. Signatures sometimes moulded on base.
  - Rosenthal still active.

ROSEVILLE

Roseville Pottery was founded in 1890 in Roseville, Ohio. Made basic, well-designed, utilitarian stoneware.

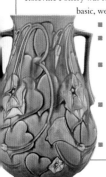

  - 1900: launched art ware range: 'Rozane'.
  - 1901: acquired second pottery in Roseville and another in Zanesville.
  - 1905: series of Rozane lines, including 'Della Robbia', designed by Frederick H. Rhead.
  - By WWI, the production of art ware ceased in favour of production wares.

  - Closed in 1954.

Rouen

CERAMICS

ROUEN

After the Poterat monopoly (50 years exclusive rights to produce faience) expired in 1694, Rouen became one of the most important centres for the production of French faience.

- Factories in the area share common style. Specialized in ewers, and plates decorated in the *style rayonnant*. Blue on white ground.
- c1720: full range of *grand-feu* colours adopted, particularly Chinese style 'famille verte'.
- c1770: enamel colours in imitation of porcelain.
- Industry declined due to competition with English creamware.
- Last factory closed 1847.

ROYAL COPENHAGEN

Formed in 1883 when Bing & Grondahl (est. 1853) and the Royal porcelain factory (est. 1775) merged.

- Under the direction of Arnold Krog, produced a successful Art Nouveau range.
- Innovative glazing/decorating techniques. Underglaze greys and blues producing naturalistic paintings of landscapes.
- Designs include the mildly erotic eg 'The Rock and the Wave', and demur figures of children.
- All pieces mass produced in slip-cast porcelain.
- Factory still active.

ROYAL DUX

Factory established in Bohemia in 1853.

- Initially produced utilitarian stoneware. Later made majolica, terracotta and faience.
- By 1898, company moved to Berlin and produced porcelain. Became known as 'Duxer Porzellan-Manufaktur'.
- Ornamental pieces, tableware and figures: nude or semi-clad nymphs.
- Mark: rose-coloured triangle with acorn and "Royal Dux Bohemia".
- Factory still in operation.

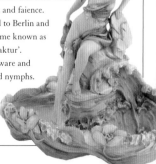

Saturday Evening Girls

SAINT-CLOUD

French factory made variety of soft paste porcelain from 1690s.

- Wares include: ice pails, spice-boxes, snuff boxes, bonbonnières. Speciality: undecorated pot-pourri vases.
- Pieces heavily potted. Glaze thick and clear, frequently showing pitting.

- Body has a yellowish tone.
- Until mid-1730s pieces mainly decorated in underglaze blue.
- After mid-1730s polychrome wares and Japanese-style wares with Kakiemon/Imari patterns.
- Standards fell from c1750. Factory closed 1766.

SAMSON

Opened in Paris in 1845, Edmé Samson's factory made copies of Chinese, German and English porcelain, French faience, Dutch Delft, and some Strasbourg wares.

- Excellent copies of Meissen and Chinese porcelain.
- English soft paste porcelain fakes easier to detect, as Continental hard paste was used.
- Claimed all wares had S within mark, but this easy to remove.
- Production ended 1969. Moulds sold 1979.

SATURDAY EVENING GIRLS

Began as an Arts & Crafts club for immigrant girls who met at the North Branch of Boston Library in 1899.

- 1906: club acquired small kiln.
- 1907: pottery opened, headed by Edith Brown. Moved to larger premises. Renamed 'Paul Revere Pottery'.
- Hand-decorated ceramics, including bowls, vases, tiles, tea-wares, dinner sets, children's breakfast sets.
- Pottery closed in 1942, as expenses could not be met.

Sèvres

SÈVRES

With the decline in popularity of Meissen in the mid-18thC, the Vincennes/Sèvres factory in France (est. 1740) became arguably the most important porcelain factory in Europe.

- First director, Claude-Humbert Gérin, made a soft paste porcelain much whiter than that of other French factories.
- 1745: Louis XV granted 20-year exclusive privilege to produce porcelain.
- Early wares heavy in form, painted with small flower sprays. Gilt trellis and scrollwork borders.
- 1748: goldsmith Jean Claude Chambellan Duplessis hired to create new Rococo forms. Lighter, more elegant shapes.
- From 1753, other factories forbidden to use Vincennes subjects, colours, and gilding by the king.
- 1756: factory moved to Sèvres, near Paris.
- 1768: hard paste porcelain. Coloured and patterned grounds. Little body left showing.
- Late 1770s: Sèvres produced strictly geometric shapes based on antique vase and urns. Subdued sepia/greys instead of bright Rococo colours. Classical motifs.
- Early 1780s: 'jewelled' (drops of enamel) decoration introduced.
- Following the Revolution, porcelain sold to be decorated in Paris and London.
- Rich 'Empire' style developed early 19thC.
- Art Nouveau style adopted in late 1890s. Art Deco in 1920s.
- Currently, produces simplified versions of 18thC wares.

SITZENDORF

In 1850, Carl and Alfred Voigt, and Wilhelm Liebmann founded a porcelain factory in Thuringia, Germany.

- Mainly decorative porcelain in Meissen style.
- Factory burnt down in 1858, but rebuilt.
- Called Gebrüder Porzellanmanufaktur from 1884-96.
- Factory still in active today under the name "VEB Sitzendorfer Porzellanmanufaktur" from 1902.

SPODE

Founded in 1776 at Stoke-on-Trent, by Josiah Spode.

- Initially produced cream-coloured earthenware.
- From 1783, very fine type of pearlware. Very smooth, excellent ground for underglaze blue.
- Fine painting and Japanese Imari patterns.
- The Willow pattern developed by Josiah Spode from an original Chinese pattern called Mandarin in about 1790.
- Many services decorated with 'bat-printed' designs. Tiny dots of oil were applied to the surface of porcelain, finely powdered colour dusted onto oil to form the design.
- Late 18thC, mimicked Wedgwood's red ware and jasper ware.
- 1805: discovered recipe for stone china: extremely hard earthenware. Ideal for statues and busts.
- Stoneware decorated with blue transfer-printed underglaze designs of oriental/Italianate views and hunting scenes.
- 1833: acquired by William Taylor Copeland, who had been a partner since 1814, and Thomas Garrett. Subsequently known as 'Copeland and Garrett'.
- Mid-19thC ware: parian ware figures; elaborate table-services decorated with meticulously painted landscapes, flowers, birds, etc; household crockery; garden furniture etc.
- Wares marked with name, impressed or painted.
- Factory still open. Known as 'Spode Ltd.' since 1970.

Strasbourg

STRASBOURG

The Strasbourg pottery and porcelain factory was founded in 1721 and was run by the Hannong family.

- Early products unambitious blue and white wares.
- Late 1750s, faience decorated in enamel colours after brothers: Christian Wilhem, Karl Heinrich and Adam Friedrich von

Löwenfink joined. These painters responsible for naturalistic flowers – known in France as *fleurs de Strasbourg*. Wares include table services, pot-pourris, clock cases etc.
- Porcelain made 1752-55.
- Factory closed in 1781 after series of bad administrators.

SWANSEA

Swansea potteries and porcelain factories were active from 1765. Most important was 'The Cambrian Pottery', founded in 1814 by Lewis Weston Dillwyn, William Billingsley and Samuel Walker.

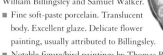

- Fine soft-paste porcelain. Translucent body. Excellent glaze. Delicate flower painting, usually attributed to Billingsley.
- Notable figure/bird paintings by Thomas Baxter.
- Swansea mark often faked.
- 1816: Billingsley left for Nantgarw (see p42).
- Porcelain factory closed 1822.
- Also active at Swansea: 'The Glamorgan pottery' c1813-39.

TECO

The American Terracotta and Ceramic Co. was founded by William Day Gates and originally produced bricks.

- 1902: Teco Art Pottery began; made vases, tiles, garden ornaments.
- Architectural shapes. Thickly potted walls, looped/buttressed handles. Minimal decoration.
- High-quality pale, silvery green matt glaze. Occasionally highlighted with metallic black overglaze.
- Ceased production in the mid-1920s.

TOURNAI

In 1750, François-Joseph Peterinck established a factory in Tournai, Belgium. Began producing soft paste porcelain.

- Meissen influence on tableware shapes. English inspired decoration. Large range of figures.
- Specialities: exotic birds/Aesop's fables in underglaze blue, landscape vignettes in purple monochrome.
- 1796: Peterinck retired. Ownership passed to daughter. Factory continued to make household wares, but no more figures.
- Many 18thC wares painted by the Hague factory.
- Factory closed mid-19thC.

TUCKER

Porcelain factory, established in 1825 by William Ellis Tucker in Philadelphia, Pennsylvania. First US porcelain factory of note.

- Early wares painted with scenes in sepia and dark brown.
- 1823: became 'Tucker & Hulme'; 'Tucker & Hemphill' in 1831.
- 1833-36: factory run by Joseph Hemphill with Tucker's brother, Thomas, as manager.
- During Hemphill period, wares became much richer. Patterns derived from Sèvres. Heavy gilding. Brightly painted flower decorations.
- Factory closed 1838.

VAN BRIGGLE, ARTUS (1869-1904)

In 1899, Artus and Anna Van Briggle relocated to Colorado Springs, Colorado, from Ohio, in the hopes of easing Artus's tuberculosis. There they founded Van Briggle Pottery.

- Organic-shaped vessels decorated with sumptuous matt glazes.
- 1900: Artus succeeded with matt glaze similar to 'dead' glaze of Chinese Ming Dynasty.
- Best wares produced before Artus' death in 1904.
- High quality art wares still produced with Anna in control. Factory sold 1912.
- Factory still active.

Wedgwood

WEDGWOOD

Founded by Josiah Wedgwood at Burslem,
Staffordshire, in 1759, can be considered
the most important English pottery.

- Began by covering wares made by
  William Greatbatch with a green
  glaze developed by Wedgwood.
- Creamware: improved version of Booth's
  cream-coloured earthenware covered in a
  cream-coloured glaze. Simple elegant
  patterns. From c1765: known as Queen's
  ware in honour of Queen Charlotte.
  Left plain or decorated with transfer
  printing/ enamel colours.
- 1769: partnership with Thomas Bently.
  'Etruria' factory opened.
- By early 1770s: developed fine-
  grained stoneware called basalt
  ware, or black basaltes. Severe
  Classical styles.
- Jasperware (from 1775): relief decorations
  in white on blue, lavender, green or yellow vases. Based on the
  shapes/decorations of Greek vases.
  Also made useful wares, such as
  teapots, jugs etc.
- 1920s: 'Fairyland' lustre: designed by
  Susannah "Daisy" Makeig-Jones (1881-
  1945). Colourful vessels decorated with elves,
  imps and pixies in idealized landscapes.
- Keith Murray (1892-1981) designed a range of simple, geometric
  forms during the 1930s: vases and bowls etc. Semi matt glazes:
  predominantly green, sometimes matt straw, Windsor grey, pale
  blue, black, or moonstone. Bears Murray's
  printed signature/initials.
- 1940: new factory at Barlastion
  opened. Continues to produce
  copies of 18thC jasper wares,
  earthenwares and bone porcelain.
- Marks: impressed "Wedgwood",
  "Wedgwood and Bently", or "WB".

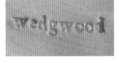

VIENNA

Porcelain factory founded in 1719 in Vienna, Austria, by Claudius Innocentius Du Paquier, with the assistance of staff from Meissen.

- Body: distinctive smoky tone, sometimes greenish. Similar to Meissen wares in form. Decoration denser: chinoiseries, *fleurs des inde*, naturalistic flowers (from 1725, before they appeared at Meissen) and extensive use of trellis work or *gitterwerk*. Baroque style.
- 1744: Du Paquier relinquished factory to the state. Factory adopted the Austrian shield as a mark.
- c1750: new patterns introduced on Rococo tablewares.
- Plain bases used from mid-1760s.
- 1784: ailing factory unsuccessfully offered for sale. Under the direction of Konrad von Sorgenthal, factory transformed into prosperous concern.
- Simple geometric forms and wares decorated in strong colours and raised gilding. Joseph Leithner (chemist from 1791) introduced a dark-blue glaze, known by his name.
- Factory closed in 1864.
- Late 19thC: other factories in

 Vienna and surrounding area producing similar wares. Style now known as 'Vienna'.

WELLER

Founded by Samuel A. Weller in Fultonham, Ohio, 1872. Initially produced utilitarian pots, soon painted wares. By 1888 moved to Zanesville and by 1893 made art ware, later known as 'Louwelsa'.

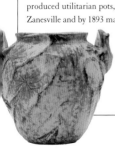

- Iridescent 'Sicado Ware' designed by Jacques Sicard.
- 'Jap Birdimal' by Frederick H. Rhead.
- By the end of WW1, production ware replaced most of Weller's better lines.
- Pottery closed in 1945.

CERAMICS

WEMYSS

Wemyss ware was produced at the Fife
Pottery, Kikcaldy, from c1883 to 1930.

- c1820: pottery founded as Robert Heron
  & Son. Run by Robert Methven Heron
  during main Wemyss production period.
- c1882: Karl Nekola in charge of painting shop.
  Introduced cabbage roses and other characteristic motifs.
- Products include wash-basins, jugs, large pigs for use as door-
  stops, variety of tablewares. Jam pots especially popular.
- Decorations include: cherries, plums, apples, etc., cottage-
  garden flowers, cocks and hens, etc.
- After 1900: production of large pieces declined.
- 1916: Edwin Sandland took over painting shop.
- Production stopped in 1930.
- Rights and moulds sold to Bovey Tracey pottery. Nekola's son
  Joseph moved there and continued to
  paint traditional Wemyss ware deco-
  rations until his death in 1942.
  - Marks: Usually factory name and
    "Nekola" if painted by him.

ZSOLNAY

In 1865, Vilmós Zsolnay purchased his brother's artisan pottery
(est. 1862) in Fünfkirchen (now Pécs), Hungary.

- Immediately started to compete with Czech and Austrian factories, by assembling highly skilled team of craftsmen.
- 1870s: imitation of Iznik ware called 'Ivoir-Fayence' decorated
  in *grand-feu* colours with porcelain glaze.
- Until 1890s: ornate pieces inspired by Islamic pierced wares.
- 1890s: Art Nouveau wares, often designed by J. Rippl-Rónai.
- 1893: Vincse Wartha became art director.
- Multicoloured iridescent glazes and lustres; most successful an
  iridescent glaze called "eosin".
- Simple, naturalistic forms. Floral and asymmetric.
- Low-relief moulded detail. Motifs include tree silhouettes and
  red skies with lustrous surface.
- Also produced crystalline
  glazes. Mineral salts added to
  glaze formed crystals that
  looked like frost.
- Vilmós Zsolnay succeeded
  by his son, Miklos. Factory
  survives as State concern.

WORCESTER

Porcelain factory founded in 1751. Took over stock and secrets of Lund's Bristol porcelain factory the following year.

- First porcelain soft paste, including soaprock (steatite).
- 1751-56: useful wares, especially tea wares, and vases. Chinoserie motifs in underglaze blue/enamel colours.
- c1751–53: blue and white and 'famille verte' polychrome wares produced.
- c1752–54: incised cross or line mark.
- c1755–60: polychrome decoration crisp and clean. Almost all patterns based on Chinese prototypes.
- Transfer printed wares appear c1757. At first overglaze in black. By 1760 also underglaze in blue.
- 1760–76: most blue and white pieces marked with crescent.
- 1760s: much rich enamel painting apparently executed outside factory.
- Post 1760s: tendency to imitate Sèvres.
- 1783: factory bought by Thomas Flight for sons, Joseph and John. Formula for paste modified.
- 1793-1807: named 'Flight & Barr'.
- 1807-14: named 'Barr, Flight & Barr'
- 1814-40: named 'Flight, Barr & Barr'.
- 1840: amalgamated with factory started by R. Chamberlain. Moved to their workshops.
- 1852: renamed 'Kerr & Binns'.
- 1862: renamed 'Royal Worcester'. Elaborate, richly gilded/painted, jewelled decoration.
- 1870s-80s: Japanese influence.
- 19thC/early 20thC: many wares decorated with rich bunches of flowers or fruit on a cream or light ground.
- Factory still active.

Ceramic Marks

CERAMICS

Amphora
Bohemia, late 19thC

Ansbach
Germany, 1765-90

Ansbach
Germany, from 1870

Batchelder
US, 1912-32

Bing & Grondhal
Denmark, 20thC

Bock Wallendorf
Germany, from 1903

Frankenthal
Germany, 1759-62

Furstenberg
Germany, 1753-70

Gotha
Germany, 1802-34

Gustavsberg
Sweden, 20thC

Herend
Hungary, 20thC

Kloster-Veilsdorf
Germany, c1760

Ludwigsburg
Germany, 1758-93

Nymphenburg
Germany, 20thC

Pilkington
UK, 1903-13

Ceramic Marks

Potschappel
Germany, from 1872

Rorstrand
Sweden, 20thC

Ruskin Pottery
UK, 1898-1933

St Petersburg
Russia, 1801-25

St Petersburg
Russia, 1855-81

Troika
UK, 1963-67

Rudolstadt-Volkstedt
Germany, from 1935

Wolfsohn, Helena
Germany, 19thC

Zurich
Switzerland, 1763-90

UNDERSTANDING MARKS

Marks on any object can be helpful when identifying the maker, date and country of manufacture. However, always exercise caution – marks are not always what they seem. The mark shown below left suggests that the item is made of Chinese porcelain. However, a closer look at the mark shows that the piece was made at a factory in Longport, Staffordshire, England. The words "Chinese Porcelaine" are probably the pattern name used by the factory. The mark below right includes the word "England". This suggests the piece was made between

1891-1921. For more information on marks see *pages 22–27*.

Cardew, Michael

CERAMICS

CARDEW, MICHAEL (1901-1983)

Cardew was an early pupil of Bernard Leach and the most prolific.

- Founded Winchcombe pottery. Rediscovered historical slip-decoration. Red earthenware.
- 1939: founded Wenford Bridge.
- 1942: taught in 1926 in West Africa and later opened the Aboja Pottery in the same area.

COPER, HANS (1920-1981)

Coper was born in Germany and moved to England in 1939.

- Worked with Lucie Rie.
- 1959: studio in Hertfordshire.
- Taught at the Camberwell School of Art and Royal College of Art.
- Vessels often derived from ancient Egyptian/Cycaldic pots. Matt black/buff-white/cream. Subtly textured.

FANTONI, MARCELLO (b. 1915)

Florentine potter who referenced Etruscan forms.

- Combined sympathy for Modern Art and Italian heritage.
- Bright or earthy colours, glazes applied in a painterly manner, rough surfaces.
- Wares distributed in US by Raymor.
- 1970: founded International School of Ceramic Arts in Florence, where he continues to work.

HAMADA, SHOJI (1894-1978)

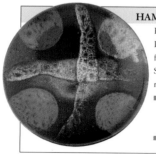

Born in Tokyo, met Bernard Leach in 1918. In 1920 they founded the Leach Pottery in St. Ives, Cornwall. Hamada returned to Japan in 1924.

- Pottery in response to simple/traditional wares of Japanese hometown.
- Used local Japanese clays.

JOUVE, GEORGE (1910-1964)

Jouve was a French ceramicist.

- Inspired by ancient European forms and modern techniques.
- Simple, geometric forms decorated with single-colour glazes. Other wares feature applied plaques.
- Used selenium, which lead to extraordinarily vibrant coloured glazes, usually red.

LEACH, BERNARD (1887-1979)

Leach studied potting techniques in Japan. He returned to England in 1920 and started the Leach Pottery in St. Ives, Cornwall with Shoji Hamada.

- Traditional Eastern-style wares with English techniques like slip decoration and salt glazing.
- Trained many of the best British studio potters, including son, David.

NATZLER

Vienna-born husband and wife team, Otto (1908-2007) and Gertrud Natzler (1908-71), moved to the US in 1938.

- Gertrud worked the wheel; Otto formulated glazes/fired the pots.
- Initially only bowls, but later gourds, bottles, reproductions of natural forms.
- Volcanic 'lava' type glazes.

OHR, GEORGE (1857-1918)

Ohr was known as the 'Mad Potter of Biloxi'.

- Referred to pots as 'mud babies'. Those rescued from a 1894 fire known as 'burnt babies'.
- Paper thin ceramic often with folded rim or in-body twist.
- Early work: complicated glazes – sometimes two or more completely different glazes per pot.
  - Post 1900: simplicity. Plain bisque, no glazes.

CERAMICS

PICASSO, PABLO (1881-1973)

Started making ceramics in 1946.

- 1947-66: worked with Suzanne and Georges Ramié, owners of Madoura.
  - Picasso designed the pieces and Suzanne Ramié fired them.
  - Figural/animal shapes painted with stylized depictions of animals/the body.

PLEYDELL BOUVERIE, KATHARINE (1895-1985)

Was a student of Bernard Leach.

- After a year at Leach Pottery, set up the Cole Pottery at Coleshill, Berkshire, in 1925. Forced to close in WW2.
- Ash-glazes. Experimented with glazes with Norah Breden.
- Simple formed vessels in a wide variety of glazes.

RIE, LUCIE (1902-1995)

Known for her post-war finely potted bottle and bowl forms.

- Although her work was intended to be functional, its architectural and often sculptural forms and wider range of less rustic, and sometimes brighter, glazes puts her work in a different league to that of Leach.
  - Typically worked in a palette of brown, beiges, greys and creams.

SCHEID, URSULA & KARL (b. 1929)

Founder members of the influential German ceramics group Keramikergruppe 83.

- Work reflects the German design aesthetic, with a tendency to precise forms, geometry and line work, and yet her forms have a great sense of fluidity and balance about them.
- 1979-92 designed for Rosenthal Studio Line.

SCHEIER

Husband and wife team Edwin
(b. 1910) and Mary Scheier (1908-
2007) made ceramics together.

- Studio in Glade Springs, Virginia.
- Taught at University of New Hampshire, US.
- 1968-78: Lived in Oaxaca, Mexico, before moving to Arizona.
- Symbols of life, death, rebirth.
- Style similar to Picasso/Klee.

STAITE MURRAY, WILLIAM (1881-1962)

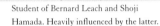

Student of Bernard Leach and Shoji Hamada. Heavily influenced by the latter.

- Interested in Oriental high-fired glazes.
- Constructed kiln at Rotherhithe, London in 1919. Attempted to re-create classical Chinese effects such as dark temmoku glaze.

VOULKOS, PETER (1924-2002)

Voulkos was an American artist of Greek descent.

- Post modern style: celebrated the raw qualities of un-worked clay.
- Pottery: torn, twisted, gouged and deliberately useless.
- Established the ceramics departments at Otis Art Institute, Los Angelese, Calif and (in 1959) at the University of California, Berkley.

WOOD, BEATRICE (1893-1998)

Wood did not become interested in ceramics until her forties.

- Moved to California in 1948.
- Pottery primarily sculptural – many vessels decorated with tiny apertures.
- Volcanic glazes in bright colours and earth tones with tiny pits.
- Applied decoration, inspired by India.

Glossary

albarello Waisted drug jar.

applied Attached, rather than modelled in the body.

baluster vase Vase which swells first out and then in to create a shape like a baluster (*see page 156*).

bellarmine Type of stoneware flagon, made in Germany from 16thC.

bat printed Transfer printed.

bianco-sopra-bianco 16thC maiolica or 18thC Delft decorated in white over a whitish-greyish ground.

biscuit Porcelain or pottery fired, but unglazed, made first in France in 18thC.

bisque French for biscuit.

blue-dash Blue dabs round the rim of a plate, found on 17thC and 18thC delftware.

bocage The bush, shrub or foliage surrounding or supporting a pottery or porcelain figure.

body The shaped clay itself, as distinct from its subsequent surface glaze or decoration.

bone china Pearlware with bone ash in the formula: almost entirely porcell-anous. Produced from just before 1800.

Castleford ware Shiny white porcellanous stoneware made in Castleford and elsewhere from c1790.

cow creamer China or silver jug or boat for pouring cream, modelled as a cow.

crazing Cracks in a glaze.

creamware Earthenware glazed in a cream or butter colour with a porcelain effect, developed by Wedgwood in the 1760s and soon widely made elsewhere.

crenellated Crinkly or wavy.

crested china Ware decorated with heraldic crests, made first by Goss and then, after 1880, by many different Staffordshire and other English and also German potteries.

delft or **delftware** Tin-glazed earthenware, often decorated in styles deriving either from Chinese porcelain or from 17thC Dutch painting. "Delftware" acceptably embraces not only ware with a Delft mark but any 17thC or 18thC pottery of the same type and style. If actually made in Holland, it is written "Delft ware" with a capital D.

Deutsche Blumen "German flowers". Loose flowers or bouquets painted on ware (e.g. from Meissen) from mid 18thC.

dry-edge With edges clear or bare of glaze.

earthenware Pottery made with porous clay which therefore requires a sealant glaze (unlike stoneware or porcelain).

écuelle French soup bowl with two handles; usually made with a cover and stand (e.g. Sèvres).

enamel colours A vitreous onglaze ceramic pigment that fuses when fired at a relatively low temperature.

Enghalskrüge Large German tin- glazed jug with a cylindrical neck.

everted Turned or curled over, e.g. a rim.

faience Tin-glazed earthen-ware (after Faenza in Italy, a maiolica centre).

fairings Porcelain figures of 19thC and 20thC made in the mould, especially in Germany. They depict genre or situation comedy, or animal figures, and usually carry descriptive captions.

famille verte, rose, jaune or noire Type of oriental porce-lain *(see page 74)*.

flatware Flat pottery or porcelain, e.g. plates, dishes, chargers etc.

frit Glassy dross, an ingredient of soft-paste porcelain; also sometimes applied with or over pottery glaze.

garniture Set of ornamental pieces of pottery or porcelain.

Goss china Range of porcelain and parian ware produced from 1858 at Stoke-on-Trent, but particularly heraldic china.

hard paste porcelain Porcelain made with kaolin and petuntse, as the Chinese produce it. First made in Europe in early 18thC at Meissen. *(See page 40)*.

Imari Type of oriental porcelain *(see page 74)*.

Indianische Blumen "Indian flowers". European imitation of the Japanese Kakiemon style, found in mid 18thC e.g. on Meissen or Höchst.

ironstone Type of stoneware patented in 1813 by Mason, in which slag from iron furnaces was mixed into the clay, tough-ening the ware.

istoriato Italian for "with a story on it", form of maiolica decoration.

jardinière A French term for a large ornamental vessel, for holding cut flowers or growing plants.

jasperware Variety of coloured stoneware developed by Wedgwood.

Glossary

lead-glazed The type of glaze first used in Western pottery, taken over perhaps from glass-making. In the 17thC refined to "liquid lead glaze" and in 18thC to "colourless lead glaze". Lead (lead sulphide) continued as an ingredient in other glazes (eg tin glaze, salt glaze).

lustre Ware of any kind decorated with a metallic coating (which changes colour when fired: eg gold becomes ruby-red).

majolica A corrupted form of the word 'maiolica' it was used from the mid 19thC for

earthenware covered in thick, colourful glazes.

overglaze A second glaze laid over the first; the pot is then fired again. May also be called "enamel".

parian Porcelain formula developed in mid 19thC by Copeland, named after Parian white marble: the figures are typically uncoloured, resembling biscuit.

pearlware A type of earthenware, whiter and shinier than creamware, produced from late 18thC by Wedgwood, Spode and others, and commonly print decorated.

petuntse See porcelain.

porcelain Porcelain is made from a clay (or paste) called kaolin (after the place in China where it is found) combined with petuntse, the Chinese term for the feldspathic rock that produces a glaze. Similar clay and rock were first found in Europe at Meissen in about 1700, making direct imitation of Chinese ware possible (hard paste porcelain); elsewhere, notably in England, there were increasingly successful attempts to reproduce the strength and translucency of oriental porcelain with substitute (soft paste porcelain). *(See pages 28-29)*.

porcellanous Having some (but not all) of the ingredients or characteristics of true porcelain.

Prattware A type of earthenware made in Staffordshire in the late 18thC and early 19thC, decorated in distinctive colours on a buff ground.

print decoration Decoration not hand-painted.

redware American clay pottery which turns red-brown when fired. Made since the 18thC, early pieces are more valuable.

reserved Kept clear, eg from painted decoration applied after glazing.

resist An area reserved from the overall decoration (usually silver or gilt).

saltglaze Type of stoneware. Salt added into the hot kiln fuses with the body to create a glassy surface approximating true porcelain. Either brown or almost white, depending on the composition of the body, saltglaze is found from c1720.

scratch blue Decoration incised or scratched, then painted blue. Found on 18thC saltglaze ware.

sgraffito From the Italian for 'little scratch', a form of decoration made by scratching through a surface to reveal a lower layer of a contrasting colour.

shoulder Outward projection of a vase under the neck or mouth.

slipware Slip is clay mixed with water. Slipware is earthenware to which slip is applied as decoration.

soft paste porcelain Porcelain in which frit or soapstone is used (instead of the petuntse of hard paste porcelain). Developed by English potters in mid 18thC.

spill vase Vase for holding spills (lighting tapers).

sponged Blurred decorative dabs, representing eg foliage. Typical of 17thC and early 18thC delft.

sprig Applied or relief ornament, not necessarily consisting of sprigs or foliage. Often made in moulds.

stoneware Any earthenware that is not porous after firing (usually due to the presence of sand or flint in the clay).

tazza Italian for "plate".

tin-glazed Earthenware with a lead glaze to which tin is added. Used for fine ware in Europe in 16thC and 17thC (eg maiolica, faience, delft).

Transfer-printing A process for decorating ceramics in which an engraved copper plate is covered with ink, prepared with metallic objects. The engraved design is then transferred to paper and while wet is pressed on to the surface of the object. The design is then fixed by firing.

underglaze Colour or design painted under or before the glaze.

wall pocket Flat-backed vase with small holes for suspension against a wall to hold flowers.

well The hollow or interior of a bowl or plate.

Introduction to Chinese Ceramics

ORIENTAL CERAMICS

- The Chinese had perfected the techniques of porcelain making during the Tang dynasty (AD618–906). The potters of the Sung dynasty (AD960–1279) made exquisite pieces for the Imperial Court, and in the Yuan dynasty (1280–1368) underglaze painting was developed.

- When buying Chinese porcelain there are certain facts you should consider. Firstly condition affects the price considerably – a very good piece with a hairline crack or small chip can be reduced in value by up to two-thirds.

- The rarity of the item is also important: rare items fetch considerably more than their common counterparts.

- It is sometimes difficult to determine the age of oriental porcelain because the patterns were repeated throughout the ages. In order to distinguish Ming porcelain from the later Qing wares, it is necessary to appreciate the technical rather than the decorative differences between the two. The Qing decorators frequently copied ancestral designs with great accuracy, therefore making it difficult to attribute certain pieces.

- With certain exceptions, Ming porcelain is more heavily glazed and the depth of glaze effects a bluish or greenish tint. Rarely is the glaze evenly applied, and if carefully examined one can detect runs and dribbles of excess glaze. Most Qing wares have a glaze of uniform thickness.

- Particularly characteristic is the pure white appearance achieved by the Kangxi potters by coating vessels in a thin and even wash.

- During the reigns of Yongzheng and Qianlong some pieces were deliberately covered in a thick glaze in order to emulate the early 15thC porcelains.

- Footrims on Ming wares were generally knife-pared and little effort was made to remove the facets left by the blade. Most, if not all, Qing pieces were smoothed after trimming.

- The feet on Ming dishes or bowls are for the most part higher than Qing examples. The footrim on Ming wares will generally manifest a narrow orange zone abutting the edge of the glaze. This is due to the presence of iron in the body of the porcelain, which appears to oxidize more strongly in the kiln in the area most closely in contact with the glaze.

- The later Chinese wares tended to be mass-produced for export, often to meet the specific demands of traders. It is

Introduction to Chinese Ceramics

on these mass-produced items that the potters frequently used the marks of earlier dynasties. This was not the work of a faker, rather the Chinese believed they should venerate the skills of

A Warring States tripod or ding. AD 475-221

previous generations. Accordingly, they marked the piece with the mark of the Emperor who was reigning at the time they wished to honour.

Dingyao

A northern Chinese porcelain produced during the Sung and Yuan periods. The rich ivory glaze is pale green or brown where it pools. Decoration is mainly floral.

Junyao

A northern Chinese stoneware made from the Sung Dynasty through to the Yuan and Ming periods. The coarse granular body has a thickly applied blue glaze, sometimes varying from lavender to deep purple.

Yingqing

A porcelain produced during the Sung and Yuan dynasties in central and southern China. The dominant characteristic is the pale blue-green translucent glaze. Like Dingyao, the designs are moulded or carved floral subjects.

The Marks

The "reign" marks found on oriental porcelain (and on other works of art) record the dynasty and the emperor's name. However, be cautious if you suspect an earlier mark has been used.

Square seal marks are sometimes used instead of the more usual character marks. The characters read from the top right down. In a six character mark, the characters therefore read: "Great", Dynasty, Emperor's first name, Emperor's second name, period made.

A Tang Dynasty, sancai pottery model of a horse.

Ming Dynasty marks

ORIENTAL CERAMICS

Chinese porcelain dates back to about 10thCAD. From then until 14thC, different regions produced their own characteristic wares. The Ming period (1368–1644) saw a remarkable growth both in quality and quantity throughout the country.

Hongwu
1368-1398

Yongle
1403-1424

Xuande
1426-1435

Chenghua
1465-1487

Hongzhi
1488-1505

Zhengde
1506-1521

Jiajing
1522-1566

Longquing
1567-1572

Wanli
1573-1619

Tianqi
1621-1627

Chongzhen
1628-1644

Qing Dynasty marks

ORIENTAL CERAMICS

At the start of the Qing Dynasty, a large part of the output was produced for the export market. Standards tended to decline during the late 18thC and 19thC, but fine quality non-export "Chinese taste" pieces continued to be produced.

Shunzhi
1644-1661

Kangxi
1662-1722

Yongzheng
1723-1735

Qianlong
1736-1795

Jiaqing
1796-1820

Daoguang
1821-1850

Xianfeng
1851-1861

Tongzhi
1862-1874

Guangxu
1875-1908

Xuantong
1909-1911

Hongxian
(Yuan Shikai)

Pronunciation, Japanese Periods

ORIENTAL CERAMICS

Standard (Mandarin) Chinese was until recently transcribed into western script (romanized) according to the Wade-Giles system devised early in 20thC . This has now been superseded by the Pinyin system which tends to give more easily under-stood phonetic values to the Chinese words being represented. The listing below should help in developing a pronunciation of Chinese terms that can be used with reasonable confidence.

Pronunciation

Pinyin	Approx. only
zh or j	as in jeans
ch or q	as in cheap or cringe
x	as in shell
r	as in rage
g or k	as in gorse or core
b	as in born
p	as in pour
d	as in door
t	as in torn
z	as in roads
c	as in tsetse

Japanese periods

cBC7,000. Jomon culture.
cBC300. Yayoi culture.
1thC to 4thCAD. Haniwa.
220AD. first influence
from Korea.
Asuka: 552–645
Hahuko: 672–685
Nara: 710–794
Heian: 794–1185
Kamakura: 1185–1333

*An Edo period Arita model
of a Karashishi. c1700*

Muromachi (Ahikaga):
1338–1573
Momoyama: 1573–1615

1598: Korean potters begin kilns at Kyushu, producing first glazed pottery in Japan.
Edo (Tokugawa): 1615–1867
1616: first porcelain made by Ninsei (1596–1666)
1661–1673: great age of porcelain; Arita, Nabeshima, Kutani and Kakiemon.
1716–1736: popularity of lacquering and netsuke.
Meiji: (1868–1912) strong influence of Western cultures. Great age of Satsuma. (*See page 74*).

*Mark on base of a Meiji
Satsuma earthenware vase.*

Shipwreck Cargoes

The great age of trade with China brought great wealth to the traders in Europe, but many crews and cargoes were lost at sea. Some of those lost ships have been raised in recent years. Their cargoes are avidly collected.

HATCHER CARGO

Dates from c1643. Cargo came on the market in 1984. The ship was probably a Chinese junk bound for Amsterdam. It was carrying 25,000 pieces of blue and white ceramics from Jingdezhen.

VUNG TAU CARGO

Dates from c1690-1700. Cargo came on the market in 1990. The ship was bound for Batavia and then Amsterdam. When it sank 48,000 pieces of Kangzi wares, mainly blue and white, were on board.

CA MAU CARGO

Dates from c1723-35. Cargo came on the market in 2007. 76,000 pieces of blue and white and other wares. Some pieces were from late Kanxi period (1662-1722), but most from Yongzheng period (1723-35).

DIANA CARGO

Dates from 1817. Cargo came on the market in 1994. 24,000 pieces of Jiaqing period (1796-1820) porcelain salvaged. Many shapes had been designed for Western-style dining. Ship was en route to India when it sank.

NANKING CARGO

Ship was called the Geldermalsen. Sank on January 3 1752. Cargo came on the market in 1986. 128,000 pieces of porcelain from the Qianlong period (1736-95) were on board, including 171 dinner services and numerous tea and coffee services. The majority of pieces are blue and white or decorated with Imari designs. Nanking is probably the most famous of the shipwreck cargoes and as such is highly desirable to collectors. Always retain the Christie's sale label – this authenticates the piece and is valued by collectors.

Imari

ORIENTAL CERAMICS

IMARI

Porcelain developed in late 17thC Japan, copied in China, Holland and the UK. Style matured c1800

- Palette includes dark underglaze blue with iron-red, gold and, sometimes, purple.
- Later wares were more densely painted.
- Majority of wares decorative.

WUCAI

A 16thC adaptation of 15thC 'doucai' decoration. It tends to be less refined with wares often carelessly painted.

- Underglaze blue as an outline or wash, with an overglaze iron-red, green, brown, yellow and black palette.
- The blue has a purple tinge.

FAMILLE JAUNE

A variation of the 'famille verte' or 'green family' of translucent enamel colours introduced in the Qing dynasty used on a yellow ground.

- The palette includes blue, green, aubergine, iron-red and black enamel colours which tend to be slightly raised.

SATSUMA

A fine Japanese earthenware with a cream-coloured ground and delicately crazed glaze decorated with overglaze enamel and gilding.

- The best pieces from the early Meiji period (1868-1912) represent the pinnacle of production.
- Finest details were painted using a single rat's hair.
- Procession scenes were popular.

Chinese Export

MING BLUE AND WHITE

From the late 14thC to c1520, Ming emperors encouraged porcelain production which resulted in the creation of stylized blue-and-white designs.

- Quality wares have a thick glaze with tiny air bubbles.
- Early designs are balanced.
- Marks were first used regularly during the Ming dynasty.

EARLY CHINESE

By 100AD a variety of ceramic wares was being made in China.

- Fine white-bodied earthenware figures are crisply modelled.
- Figures were unglazed, decorated with pigment or a three-coloured glaze known as 'sancai'.
- Funerary figures were common.

KAKIEMON

Kakiemon wares were first produced at Arita in Japan in the mid-17thC.

- Distinctive palette of iron red, deep sky blue, yellow, aubergine, turquoise green and black enhanced the milky white body.
- Wares are often of geometric form.

CHINESE EXPORT

From the 16thC, a wide range of porcelain was made and decorated in China for export to Europe.

- Generally decorative but lacks the symbolic significance of wares that were produced for the home market.
- European shapes include figure models, animals and birds. Engravings were used as a guide.

Glossary

an hua "Secret" decoration of Chinese ware, lightly incised and visible only when held up to the light.

Ao Kutani "Green" Kutani ware.

Arita Capital of a district in Japan known for its kilns; famous in particular for a type of ware known as Imari after the port from which it was shipped.

blanc-de-chine European term for the clear-glazed white porcelain made in China at Dehua in Fukien province, imported to Europe from 17thC and widely imitated in 18thC. It is remarkable for its sharp modelling and famous for its figures with swirling drapery.

bulb bowl Smallish bowl, about 12in (30cm) across for growing bulbs in, typically with three feet.

celadon European name for a Chinese ware famous for its greyish or olive green glaze (though other colours occur), usually laid over a relief or incised pattern. While celadon from the southern province of Chekiang, the original celadon, has a distinctive deep red body, Northern and other celadon has body of a

brown or other colour. First developed under the Song dynasty; but Song pieces are extremely rare.

Chinese export porcelain Porcelain made in China for the European (and later American) market. The Chinese copied both the forms and the decoration of European ware, though usually either one or the other; they copied the shapes as early as the late 16thC, and later even copied European chinoiserie decoration.

Chinese Imari Chinese imitations of Japanese Imari. Made from early

18thC, almost as early as the true Imari.

clair-de-lune A translucent blue glaze introduced in Chinese porcelain in the early 18thC.

Glossary

clobber To enamel over original blue-and-white ware with glazes of different colour.

dog of Fo Mythical Chinese lion-spaniel, a guardian spirit of the temple of the Buddha (Fo).

doucai In Chinese, "contrasting colours", a type of enamel decoration introduced in the reign of the Ming emperor Chenghua (1465–87).

famille jaune Variety of famille verte, with a yellow ("jaune") ground.

famille noire Variety of famille verte with a black ground.

famille rose 19thC European term for a Ming style of porcelain introduced at the end of the reign of Kangxi (died 1722) – a little later than "famille verte". It is polychrome, but features a rose-pink of European origin.

famille verte 19thC European term for a Ming style of porcelain (reign of Kangxi, 1662–1722). It is

polychrome, but features a brilliant copper-green.

Fukugawa Japanese ceramic company, based in Arita. Said to have been founded in 1689, but only 19thC ware is common.

gorgelet Drinking vessel with spouts or jets, made in China and Japan for export from 17thC.

Guanyin Chinese Buddhist

goddess of mercy, a favourite subject.

Guan yao Chinese term meaning "imperial ware". Song dynasty. Glazed thickly but more smoothly and regularly than other Song dynasty ware, often with a crackle, blue or grey. Now found only in 18thC copies.

Hirado Blue-and-white ware made exclusively for the Lords of Hirado, near Arita (Japan), from mid 18thC to mid 19thC. Renowned for its milk-white body, its velvety glaze, and its exquisite figure and landscape decoration.

Imari Japanese porcelain made in or around Arita from early 18thC and shipped to Europe from the port of Imari. It has distinctive colours of blue, red and gold (often with others); commonly, it is decorated in a flower-basket pattern.

Glossary

imperial yellow A distinctive yellow enamel developed in the Chinese imperial kilns in 15thC.

Jian yao Ware from Jian in Fukien province, known for its mottled brown or "hare's fur" glaze. Song and later.

Jizhou yao Ware resembling Ting ware, from Jizhou, Song dynasty.

Jun yao Ware from Jun in Honan province, with an opalescent glaze typically thick at the foot and thin at the rim. Song dynasty and later.

Kaga The district in which Kutani ware was made.

Kakiemon Name of a succession of Japanese potters, of whom the first, Kakiemon I Sakaida, died in 1666. The name stands for ware of distinctive colours and pattern, imported to Europe and widely imitated there after 1650: a brilliant azure, a soft red, yellow (and others) over a white body; delicate figures brush-drawn in

asymmetrical compositions.

Ko Kutani See Kutani.

Kraak porcelain Dutch term meaning porcelain raided from Portuguese ships called carracks. It describes the earliest kind of Chinese export porcelain (late 16thC to early 17thC), in blue and white.

Kutani Japanese ware made at Kutani in the province of Kaga in 17thC (Ko or "old" Kutani), and revived in 19thC. It is difficult to tell from Imari ware, though the Japanese value it more highly. Ao or green Kutani is a distinct stoneware, painted

in green, yellow and purple.

kylin See qilin.

Kyoto Capital of Shogunate Japan, and a centre of porcelain production in 19thC.

lang yao See sang-de-boeuf.

Li shui Chinese term for ware of celadon type. Song dynasty.

lingzhi A floral motif, found on Chinese porcelain from the reign of Jiajing (16thC).

meiping Chinese for "prunus", describing a common type of Ming flower-vase, of baluster shape, with a high shoulder, small neck and narrow mouth.

mon Japanese crest or coat of arms.

potiche French name for an oriental vase-shaped jar, usually with a cover.

Pu-Tai Chinese luohan or disciple of the Buddha,

known as "the laughing Buddha"; he has a bag of happiness.

qilin Mythical Chinese creature (also ch'ilin, kylin) with head of a dragon, limbs and body of a deer and the tail of a lion: symbol of good.

raku Pottery bowl associated with the Japanese tea-ceremony, prized for its almost rough simplicity.

sang-de-boeuf Brilliant red glaze developed in the reign of Kangxi (early 18thC), characteristic of a ware called "lang" in Chinese.

Satsuma Leading Japanese port, known also for its ware, commonly with a crackle glaze.

shishi Chinese or "Buddhist" mythical lion (also called dog of Fo).

six-character mark Six Chinese characters naming the reigning emperor, found on the base of imperial ware from the early 15thC (Xuande) to the early 18thC (Kangxi). Thereafter an archaic script is often found instead of characters. *See pages 70-71 for Chinese dynasties and marks.*

sleeve vase Vase of long thin tubular shape.

ting yao Variety of Song porcelain. The glaze, commonly white, called gummy or fatty by the Chinese, is rich and oily, with an ivory tone.

tokkuri Bottle for sake.

Transitional Wares produced between the end of the Ming, and the establishment of the Qing, dynasties.

wucai Ware of "five colours" or, often, more than five, either enamelled (over-glazed) or single-fired. Ming and Transitional.

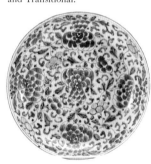

yao Kiln or ware: eg Jian yao, ware from Jian.

yen yen European term (perhaps taken from the Chinese word "yen", meaning beautiful) for a baluster vase with a long, broad flaring neck.

Yue yao Ware from Yue in Chekiang province, mostly undecorated, a forerunner of Song celadon.

Introduction

GLASS

Glass has been made since Roman times, and many techniques used then are still used today. Much glass is unmarked, often making identification difficult. Consider different forms, decoration and colours, as well as any techniques used to help you identify a maker or designer. Aim to handle as many identified examples as possible, as this will also help you. Always buy from reputable sources, willing to provide a full, descriptive receipt.

- Fashion dictates prices as much as age and intrinsic quality. Good art glass such as that by Tiffany, Lalique, or the top makers on Murano fetches the best prices.
- High prices can also be paid for mid 19thC paperweights, 18th century wine glasses and original enamelled "Mary Gregory" glasses. By comparison, 18thC Continental glass is underrated and good value. Studio glass has begun to rise in popularity.

- Most coloured decorative glass is unlikely to be

A green Roman club-shaped vase, blue iridescent overlay.

older than the 19thC. Until c1860 its use was mainly restricted to bottles, decanters and tumblers. After that date its use spread.

- The presence of bubbles is no indication of age; many pieces are 20thC.
- The earliest lead glass, c1676, has a greenish tinge; it becomes progressively more transparent and colourless until the 19thC.
- Strong lead glass, which lends itself to cutting, etching and engraving, was the predominant material in use in England from the early 18thC, but several decades later in Europe and the US.
- Lead glass has a pleasing ring when tapped with

A red overlay glass rummer, engraved by Carl Gunther.

the fingernail, though thicker pieces may not have this characteristic.

■ Lead glass has a bluish tinge under ultra-violet light; however, not all lead glass is necessarily old. Glass which looks yellow to brown under ultra-violet light, or stays the same colour, is unlikely to

A Daum cameo glass vase, vine and applied snail decoration.

be old. Oxidated pieces do not respond to this test.

■ Most genuine 18thC tableware has a pontil mark on the base. If it has been ground off there may be a polished circle where it was removed. A pontil mark is no guarantee of age, so look for other clue such as form or technique.

■ Old glass should show

A Tiffany internally-decorated carved Favrile glass vase.

other signs of the manufacturing process; look for vertical creases in the bowl, and a nick or lump in the rim where surplus glass was sheared off. Lack of these marks is cause for suspicion.

■ The foot of genuine early glass should be wider than the rim. Any repairs that destroy this proportion, such as grinding to remove a chip, considerably reduce the value.

■ To detect recent engraving place a white handkerchief inside the glass. Old engraving looks grey, and is darker than the surrounding glass. New engraving looks too white and powdery.

■ Genuine Jacobite and Williamite glass is generally restrained and subtle in its display of engraved political symbols. A proliferation of motifs suggests it was added later.

How Glass Is Made

HAND BLOWN

Glass blown and formed by hand is unique in its size, form and pattern, although examples may look similar.

- Tools such as calipers, pads and cup-shaped or other moulds may be used.
- Forms may have 'faults' or be slightly irregular, which show how they were made.
- A piece may be made of more than one section – look for a line indicating a join, such as between the stem and the foot.
- Look on the base for a pontil mark (left). This is the 'broken' area where the piece was snapped off the glassmaker's rod.

MOULD BLOWN

Glass is blown into a metal or wooden mould, with the hot molten glass picking up the raised pattern on the inside of the mould. Mould blowing allowed glass to be mass-produced both economically and consistently.

- Not all mould blown glass was or is inexpensive – Lalique used moulding and pressed techniques.
- It allows for patterned, textured surfaces to be created easily. Thin lines other than the pattern are left by joins in moulds
- Run your hand inside to find depressions and raised areas matching the design on the exterior.
- The glass is often of generally the same thickness over the entire body of the piece, and the body is a single piece.
- The base may be flat or be slightly concave, usually with no pontil mark. Moulded glass could also be finished by hand.

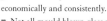
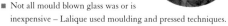

MOULDED

Factories also spin glass in a mould at high speed to ensure an even thickness of glass across the body of the piece.

- Technique used to create most mass-produced tableware today.
- Single piece, complex forms may be created consistently.
- Many moulded pieces have a machine-cut and polished rim.

How Glass Is Made

PRESSED

Much pressed glass was made to imitate more expensive cut lead crystal.

- Molten glass is manually or mechanically pressed or injected into textured moulds.
- Feel the design, which will feel rounded and less 'sharp' that cut designs. Look for mould lines.
- More complex designs that cannot be easily cut, such as floral and scrolling motifs, may be moulded.

COLOUR IN BATCH

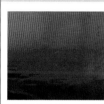

Glass can be coloured by adding chemicals or powdered enamels to the molten glass mixture, which is known as the 'batch'.

- Tone or depth of colour can vary with amount of colourant added, or the thickness of the glass.

APPLIED COLOUR

Glass can also be coloured by rolling it in powdered enamels when hot.

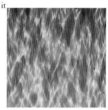

- Small chips or fragments of glass can be used to create a pattern.
- Heating the mass in the furnace melts and fuses it together.
- Chemicals can also be added to change or modify the colour.

COLOURED PATTERNS

The surface can also be worked with tools when still hot and molten, allowing patterns within the glass to be created.

- Two or more colours may be used.
- The glass may also be pulled or combed (left) to create a pattern.
- This was a popular technique during the Art Nouveau period.

Decoration

GLASS

CUTTING

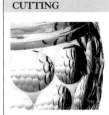

Designs tend to be geometric, based on repeated linear, oval or rounded motifs. The more complex and deep the cutting, the more valuable.

- Edges sharper to the touch than pressed glass. Damage is nearly always impossible to restore.

ENGRAVING

Glass is removed using a spinning thin copper disc, scratched, tapped or carved away with a metallic or diamond-tipped point.

- Often combined with cutting.
- More intricate designs with greater detail can be created than with cutting.
- The effect can be achieved with acid, but designs lack the quality and detail of hand-cut examples.

ENAMELLING

Metallic oxides combined with ground glass and oil are painted onto a surface, then fused by heating.

- 'Cold' enamelling is not heated in the furnace and can rub off easily.
- Different colours require different temperatures to make them permanent, meaning that enamelling can be complex.

GILDING

Gold leaf or a mixture of gold powder and fixative are applied to a surface.

- The bond is made permanent by heating. Less expensive pieces decorated 'cold'; this can rub off.
- Gold leaf may also be sandwiched between two layers of glass – this is known as Zwischengoldglass.

Decoration

IRIDESCENCE

Introduced in the 1890s and inspired
by buried Roman glass that had
changed colour over time. Used on
art and Carnival glass.

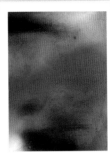

- Metallic salts are added to the
  glass, or sprayed or 'fumed' on.
- A surface effect like oil spilled in
  water is revealed in the light.
- The effect changes depending on
  glass colour and quantity of salts.
  Surface patterning also used.

CASED

Glass comprised of two or more
layers of differently coloured glass,
often with an outer colourless layer.

- A bubble of molten glass of one
  colour is coated with a differently
  coloured layer, or blown into a cup
  shape of another colour.

CAMEO

Two of more layers of coloured glass
are cut, leaving a raised pattern.

- The more layers used, the more
  valuable a piece is likely to be.
- Only removing part of a layer
  leaves graduated tones of colour.
- Acid also used; pieces lack quality
  and detail of hand-cut designs.

APPLIED

A separate, smaller mass of molten
glass is dripped onto the body of a
piece when it is being formed. Tools
are used to control flow and shape.

- Tends to have smooth, round
  edges unless it is further worked.
- Two glasses bond as they cool, but
  line will be visible.
- Used for handles, feet, decoration.

Art Glass

AMBERINA

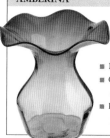

Patented in 1883 by John Locke for the New England Glass Co., Cambridge, Massachusetts. Amberina shades from light yellow-amber to ruby.

- Made 1883-c1900, but revived later.
- Colloidal gold added to mixture gives colouring. Reheated parts turn ruby.
- Reverse (ruby at base) and particularly plated (opaque lined) versions scarce.

PEACHBLOW

Made by several US and European factories as an imitation of the peach bloom glaze found on some Chinese (Kangxi) porcelain.

- Made from the early 1880s onwards.
- Typically shades from opaque white/cream/grey to rose/purple.

BURMESE

Translucent ware, shading from pink to yellow. Painted designs known.

- Made by adding uranium to batch.
- Patented by Frederick Shirley in 1881 for Mt. Washington Glass Co., US.
- Made at Thomas Webb & Sons, England, from 1886 as "Queen's Burmese".

CRANBERRY

Cranberry glass has been made in Britain, Europe and the US since the mid 19thC.

- Transparent, reddish-pink.
- Made by adding gold to batch. Reheated till colour developes.
- Later glass made using copper instead of gold, resulting in a harsher amber-red tint.
- Popular as layer in overlay glass.
- Frequently used for tablewares.

Art Glass

CRACKLE

Developed by the Venetians during the 16thC. Made by plunging hot glass into cold water and reheating and blowing into the desired shape.

- Network of fine cracks.
- Made in most colours and as colourless glass.
- Some of the best made by Sandwich and Hobbs, Brockunier & Co. (both US).

VASELINE

A transparent yellowish-green glass made by adding uranium oxide to the glass formula. Pressed and blown objects made.

- First introduced 1876 by Gillinder & Sons, Philadelphia, Pennsylvania.
- Changes colour under different lights – fluoresces under ultraviolet light.
- Height of popularity from 1860s-1890s.

SATIN

Refers to all glass with velvety/satin finish. Glass is dipped in hydrofluoric acid to create the effect.

- 1858: formulated by Benjamin Richardson, UK.
- Produced from 1886 by Mount Washington, South Boston, MA and Phoenix Glass Co., Pennsylvania, US.
- Shaded tones of rose, yellow, or blue. Also monochrome, colourless, or cased.

CROWN MILANO

Formulated by Frederick Shirley, in 1884, at Mt. Washington Glass Co., South Boston, MA.

- Made of opaque ivory coloured glass, with satin surface finish created with acid.
- Embellished by hand with brown, beige or gold floral and foliate designs, often including animals and other motifs.
- Popular until 1890s. Glossy version known as 'Shiny Crown Milano'.

Drinking Glasses

GLASS

ANATOMY OF AN 18ᵗʰC GLASS

Bowl

Collar

Knop — *Above: Folded foot, seen from below.*

Stem

Foot

- Look for a grey tinge to the glass, amber or brown tinged glass may indicate a 20thC reproduction.
- Look for joins between the bowl and the stem and/or the stem and the foot, examples made from a single piece are 20thC reproductions.
- The groups on these pages were compiled by E. Barrington Haynes in his book "Glass Through The Ages", first published by Penguin Books in 1948, and have become standard.
- Each group represents a type of stem, with sub-groups based on the shape of the bowl or the shape or decorative nature of the stem.
- Dates shown represent the main dates of popularity of a certain group.

Group I
Baluster
c1685-1725

Group II
Moulded Pedestal
c1715-65

Group III
Balustroid
c1725-60

Stems

Group IV
Light (Newcastle)
c1735-65

Group V
Composite
c1745-75

Group VI
Plain Straight
c1740-75

Group VII
Air Twist
c1745-70

Group VII
Hollow
c1750-60

Group IX
Incised (grooved spiral)
c1750-65

Group X
Opaque White Twist
c1755-80

Group XI
Mixed & Colour Twist
c1755-80

Group XII
Facet Cut
c1760-1810

Other Drinking Glasses & Stems

*Late 19thC
Tavern Rummer*

*Slice Cut Rummer
c1820s*

*Early 19thC
Rummer*

*Late 19thC
Champagne*

*Early 19thC
Ale*

*Late 18thC Jelly
(Dessert)*

*Late 18thC
Dram*

*Mid 18thC
Firing*

*Multiple Spiral
Air Twist*

Mercury Air Twist

*Mixed Opaque
& Air Twist*

*Gauze and
Single Ply Spiral*

*Pair of Spiral
Gauzes*

Colour Twist

GLASS

Knops

Air Beaded

Inverted Baluster

True Baluster

Annulated

Blade

Cushioned

Simple Knop

Faceted

Annular

Swollen

Angular (here with internal bubble)

Propeller

Bobbin

Opaque Twist

Bowls

GLASS

Bell (joined to stem, here with collar)

Bell with solid base (joined to stem)

Waisted (no join)

Thistle with solid base

Trumpet

Trumpet

Conical

Round Funnel

Ovoid

Ogee

Bucket

Saucer or Pan Top

Decanters

Shoulder
c1740-60

Perpendicular
Gothic Revival
c1840-60

Prussian
c1790-c1830

Bludgeon
c1835-80

Conical
early 19th century

Ship's
c1770-c1930

Barrel
c1780-c1830
and later

Shaft & Globe
c1730-50 and
c1850-80

Claret Jug

Barovier, Ercole

GLASS

BAROVIER, ERCOLE (1889-1974)

Barovier joined his family's glassworks (est. 1878) on Murano, Italy, in 1919.

- 1929: developed 'Primavera' with white crackled effect, black/blue trim.
- Mid-1930s: new technique colouring glass while hot without fusing.
- 1936: Merged with Ferro Toso. Now known as 'Barovier & Toso'.
- 1950s-60s: vivid colours combined with pattern. 'Intarsio' with applied sections of glass, or bubbly 'Efeso'.

BLENKO, WILLIAM (1854-1933)

Blenko founded glassworks in 1922 in West Virginia.

- Made stained glass until late 1920s when began producing domestic/ornamental glass.
- Vivid single colours in blues, reds and yellows. Also produced an amberina range.
- Designers include Winslow Anderson from 1947-52, Wayne Husted from 1952-63, and Joel Philip Myers from 1963-72.
- Bold, extravagant forms.
- Still active today.

DAUM FRÈRES

In 1885, Jean-Louis Auguste and Jean-Antonin Daum took over their father's glass factory.

- Art Nouveau/cameo glass produced from the early 1890s.
- Inspired by Emile Gallé, nature and the countryside, images from the East.
- Innovative techniques: mottled or martelé backgrounds, enamel details, patterns at various depths (intercalaire), foil-backed decoration.
- 1920s: Art Deco style: simpler shapes, geometric acid-etched patterns.
- 1920s/30s: lamps with glass shades and metal mounts by Louis Majorelle and Edgar Brandt. Also cameo landscape vases.
- Company still active today.

GLASS

GALLÉ, EMILE (1846-1904)

A pioneer of the Art Nouveau style. Set up his first decorating workshop in 1873, in Nancy, France.

- Inspired by historical cameo glass. Used up to five coloured layers. From c1899, acid etched cameo pieces also made.
- Combined cameo with enamelling, mould casting, marquetry inlay. Trapped inclusions of coloured glass/metal foils in glass.
- High quality, strongly naturalistic decoration incorporating flowers, vines, thistles, insects, plants, trees and fossils.
- A star by Gallé's name indicates production after his death.
- 1910s-20s: Acid etched vases and lamps with simpler forms and little hand finishing. Factory closed in 1936.

HOLMEGAARD

Danish glassworks founded in 1825 on Zealand.

- Began by making bottles and tableware.
- Late 1920s-1940s: Austere, functional designs in sober colours by Jacob Bang (1899-1965).
- Early 1940s-50s: flowing, organic, free blown designs in pale blues, greys and greens by Per Lütken (1916-98). See 'Beak' vase (left).
- 1960s: Angular/geometric shapes in opaque bright 'Pop Art' colours, like 'Carnaby' series.
- Factory now part of Royal Scandinavia Group.

IITTALA

Founded Finland, 1881. Began by making bottles and tableware.

- Merged with Karhula in 1917.
- 1935: 'Savoy' vase designed by Alvar Aalto – still produced today.
- 1950s-70s: Tapio Wirkkala (1915-85) and Timo Sarpaneva (1925-2005) designs: inspired by nature and Scandinavian landscape, often with textured surfaces, eg: 'Finlandia' (right).
- Company still active today.

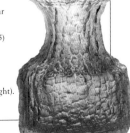

Kosta Boda

GLASS

KOSTA BODA

Kosta founded in 1742 in Småland, Sweden.

- Began making window and domestic glass. 1929: Elis Bergh appointed art director – renaissance for Kosta.
- 1950: Vicke Lindstrand (1904-83) joined.
- 1950s-60s: Curving, organic forms with thick bodies, often with internal threading or engraved designs. Also Graal and Ariel.
- Mergers: Boda in 1964, Orrefors in 1990.
- Now part of Royal Scandinavia Group.

LALIQUE, RENÉ (1860-1945)

Known as a master jeweller. Began experimenting with glass-making in Paris, France, in 1890s.

- c1907: First produced perfume bottles for François Coty, then for other Parisian perfumeries
- 1909: Bought first glassworks, acquiring another in 1918. Produced both pressed and mould blown opalescent and (scarcer) coloured glass.
- Stylized designs inspired by nature typically cover simple forms. May be stained with enamel paint to highlight details.
- 1920s-30s: designed vases, bowls, drinking glasses, perfume bottles, lamps and 28 car mascots, many in the Art Deco style.
- Quality and crispness of moulding, and virtuosity of designs give mass-produced pieces a 'one off' feel.
- Inspired imitators, such as Sabino. Fakes also known.
- Most pieces marked "R. Lalique" before his death, and "Lalique" afterwards. Lalique et Cie company still operating.

LOETZ

Glass factory founded by Johann Baptist Eisner in 1836.

- 1852: taken over by Suzanna Loetz, widow of a glass entrepreneur.
- The company was renamed "Glasfabrik Johann Loetz Witwe" and continued under this name until it closed in 1947.
- Late 1890s-c1905: Wide range of iridescent Art Nouveau glass, much exported to US.

ORREFORS

Founded in 1898 in Småland, Sweden.

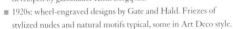

- Began making bottles and domestic glassware.
- 1916: glassmakers from Kosta join and Simon Gate (1883-45) appointed as designer – art glass production began. Edward Hald (1883-1980) joins in 1918.
- 1916: innovative Graal technique developed by glassmaker Knut Bergqvist.
- 1920s: wheel-engraved designs by Gate and Hald. Friezes of stylized nudes and natural motifs typical, some in Art Deco style.
- 1930s: Vicke Lindstrand (1904-83) designed thick-walled, clear glass vessels with optical effects and wheel-engraved motifs.
- Ariel technique (above) developed by Lindstrand, Bergqvist and Edvin Öhrström in 1937. Reputation for innovative techniques continued later with 'Kraka', 'Ravenna' and 'Fuga' ranges.
- Other notable designers include Sven Palmqvist and Nils Landberg from 1927-72, and Ingeborg Lundin from 1947-71.
- 1990: Merged with Kosta Boda and Afors.
- Factory now part of Royal Scandinavia Group.

RIIHIMÄKI

Founded in 1910 in Finland, producing bottles, tableware and window glass.

- 1930s: Carnival and some art glass made.
- Postwar designers include Helena Tynell, Nanny Still and Tamara Aladin.
- 1960s-70s: produced brightly coloured, angular and geometric moulded forms, some textured. Factory closed in 1990.

SEGUSO VETRI D'ARTE

Established in 1933 on Murano, Italy.

- 1934: Flavio Poli made art director with Archimede Seguso as master blower.
- 1940s: 'sommerso' technique developed. Brightly coloured, shell-shaped "Conchiglie" and elliptical "Valva" vases. Also "Siderale" and "Astrale" with rings.
- 1992: Production discontinued.

Notable Makers

STEUBEN

Co-founded in 1903 by Frederick Carder (1863-1963) and Thomas G. Hawkes in Corning, New York, US.

- Carder designed over 6,000 glass shapes in over 100 finishes.
- 1904-33: iridescent "Gold Aurene" (left) art glass produced. Other colours also made.
- 1905: "Verre de Soie" with silky, silvery iridescence launched. Other coloured ranges followed.
- 1933: new colourless lead-crystal '10M glass' introduced. Coloured glass phased out.
- 1930s: Engraved and cut designs, many in Art Deco style.
- Most pieces unmarked, but may have "Steuben" acid stamp or fleur-de-lys mark.
- Company still active.

TIFFANY

In 1879, Louis Comfort Tiffany (1848-1933) founded his first company.

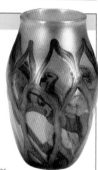

- 1880s: interior decoration, stained glass windows and lighting fixtures.
- 1885: The Tiffany Glass Co. set up in Brooklyn to make glass. Later, he founded other factories nearby.
- 1892-94: developed and launched Art Nouveau style "Favrile" iridescent glass, inspired by Roman glass.
- Simple and organic, flower or bud forms.
- Single hue (eg; gold or blue) is most common. Red is the rarest. Combinations also produced. Decoration included trademark 'peacock pattern', and also feathering and trailing.
- 1890s-1920s: different companies set up and names changed. Complex, high quality ranges introduced.
- 1900s-1920s: lamps with leaded glass shades. Brightly coloured floral and natural themes, in stylized or geometric patterns. Naturalistic bronze bases. Each unique. Reproductions common.
- Marks on base of glass include "LCT" and "Favrile" in script.
- Tiffany withdrew from glass production by 1928.

FRATELLI TOSO

Founded in 1854 on Murano, Italy.
Famous for murrines.

- Lighting, tableware, elaborate
  glass in Italian Art Nouveau style.
- 1953: 'Stellato' series launched,
  designed by Pollio Perelda.
- Late 1950s: black 'Nerox' range
  designed by Ermanno Toso.
- Company still active today.

VENINI

Founded in 1925 by Paolo Venini on
Murano, Italy.

- Handkerchief vase designed 1948-49.
- 1950s: developed many innovative techniques including "Pezzato" (right).
- Designers include Carlo Scarpa from
  1934-47, Fulvio Bianconi from 1947,
  and Tapio Wirkkala from 1966-72.
- Company still active.

WEBB, THOMAS (1804-1869)

Stourbridge glassworks known as
Thomas Webb & Sons by 1859.

- Late 19thC: coloured art glass
  and cameo ranges (left). Latter
  with clear glass and at least one
  colour (eg: red, blue, white).
- 1930s-50s: known for cut designs,
  some by David Hammond.
- Closed in 1990.

WHITEFRIARS

In 1834, James Powell acquired a
London glassworks. Closed 1980.

- Late 19thc: Venetian inspired
  and Art Nouveau style art glass.
- Pre-war designers include James
  Hogan and Harry Powell.
- Bold, colourful post-war style
  established by Geoffrey Baxter.

Pressed Glass

GLASS

- Mass production of pressed glass was developed in the 1820s and the processes are still used today.
- Molten glass is poured into a textured mould and pressed with a plunger as it cools, thus taking on the texture.
- Pressed glass can be found in transparent and opaque colours, and combinations of colours. Colourless, clear glass is the most common.
- It was typically used for inexpensive, decorative and functional household items.
- Most designs, particularly from the 19thC and early 20thC, imitated more expensive cut glass. As a result, complex linear patterns, facets and hobnails are common.
- Intricate curving designs that are hard to cut were also made.
- Makers include New England Glass and Boston & Sandwich (US), and Sowerby and Davidson (UK).

A Sowerby pressed 'malachite' glass candlestick. c1880

- Pressed glass with an opaque, marbled effect is known as 'slag' glass and was popular from c1880-1900.
- It was made by mixing waste slag into the glass mix, with purple and white being a common combination.
- During the 1920s and 1930s, designs in the Art Deco style were introduced. Makers included Bagley and Jobling (UK), and Walther (Germany).
- Translucent, streaked and marbled 'cloud glass' was also made at this time, mainly by Davidson.

A 1930s Jobling 'Dancing Girl & Block' centrepiece. c1935

Pressed Glass

A 1930s 'Royal Lace' pattern Depression glass trio set.

- One of the most common types of early 20thC pressed glass was Depression Glass, so-named after the 'Great Depression' of the 1930s. It primarily comprised inexpensive tablewares in

A 1920s Northwood purple Carnival glass rose bowl.

bright colours such as green, pink and yellow, but decorative pieces were also made. Makers included Anchor Hocking, Jeanette and Indiana.

- Also popular was Carnival glass, which gained this name as it was often given away as prizes at fairs. Popular from the 1900s-30s, it had an iridescent surface.
- Hundreds of patterns were produced by makers including Fenton, Imperial amd Northwood (US), and Sowerby (UK). Colours include the common Marigold, as well as Amethyst, and the scarcer blue. Some pieces were modified by hand after they had been pressed.
- Always consider the form carefully. The vase below has been mould blown, rather than pressed. The rim has then been modified by hand.

A Fenton Cranberry 'Coin Dot' tall vase. 1947-64

Glossary

GLASS

air-beaded Glass holding transparent bubbles of air resembling beads.

air-twist Twisting, spiral pattern formed in the glass by an enclosed bubble. Technique evolved in England from c1740 to c1770. In that period the spirals become increasingly complex.

ale glass 18thC drinking glass with long stem and tall, thin bowl, which may be engraved.

annulated Ringed.

Baccarat Factory in northern France founded in 1765 and famous for tableware and mid-19thC paperweights.

Beilby glass The Beilby family in Newcastle were the leading and most influential English painters and enam-ellers of glass in the 18thC, working until 1778.

Berluze A tall vase with an egg-shaped body and elongated, narrow neck, introduced by Daum c1900.

Boda A Swedish glass factory founded in 1864, and merged with Kosta and Afors in 1964.

Bohemia An historic area of central Europe, roughly making up the Western two-thirds of today's Czech Republic.

Bottle glass Coloured glass used for utensils such as bottles, as distinct from qualty or colourless glass.

Bristol Glass A general term given to much coloured British glass, often blue,

dating from late 18thC to the mid 19thC. Produced in and around Bristol, as well as in other British glassmaking centres, pieces include bottles, decanters, pitchers and drinking glasses.

cast glass Glass heated and shaped in a mould.

champagne glass Today, a tall glass little resembling 18thC originals, which had a shallow double-ogee bowl.

Glossary

Clichy Factory set up in 1837, in Clichy, France. Famous for paperweights

with millefiori patterns made until the 1860s.

coin glass Glass or goblet with a coin inserted in the knop of the stem. Originating in England, early 18thC.

cordial glass Glass evolved in 17thC, with a small bowl for a strong drink.

crystal glass *See lead crystal.*

cullet Scraps of glass, used to help fuse new glass.

diamond-cut Cut in diamond or lozenge shapes.

double-ogee bowl Bowl of drinking glass with a complex curved profile, resembling a larger bowl with an S-profile above a smaller one.

dram glass Small short-stemmed glass, usually, with a small rounded bowl, the

lower portion of which is normally solid.

enamel Coloured, painted decoration, fired on the glass

– ancient technique revived by the Venetians in 15thC.

facet-cut Glass cut criss-cross into straight-edged planes or facets, popular c1760-c1810.

filigrana (filigree) Glass with coloured thread-like pattern. Developed in 16thC Venice.

firing glass Thick, sturdy 17thC glass with short stem and solid foot, made to withstand drinking toasts.

flash Second layer of glass, typically incised or cut, laid over the inner glass.

flute glass Glass with tall, slender bowl. Evolved in the Netherlands in the 17thC.

Hyalith glass Opaque glass, either sealing-wax red or jet black, made respectively in Bohemia from 1803 and 1817.

May be marbled and is often gilded or enamelled.

inclusion Flaw, fault or mark in precious stones or glass.

lead-crystal Glass with lead in it which has a special brilliance. Developed for cut glass made in England and Ireland in 18thC.

lustre Term for a glass chandelier drop, or a table or mantelpiece candlestick with similar drops.

Glossary

GLASS

martelé Hammer-textured. A decorative effect used on metalwares and created using a small hammer. The same effect is created on glass by cutting small sections from the surface. Used on some Daum cameo pieces.

mercury twist An air-twist of silvery colour.

milk glass Glass made with tin oxide, which turns it an opaque white. Developed in 15thC Venice, where it was known as "lattimo". Technique soon reached Bohemia and remained popular in Germany until 19thC.

millefilli Italian term meaning a thousand threads, a type of glass made up of dozens of very fine canes.

millefiori Multi-coloured or mosaic glass. In a process known since classical times different-coloured threads of glass were laid together to make a rod that was then sectioned. Today seen most commonly in glass marbles and paperweights.

mixed-twist With opaque twists of more than one colour.

Nailsea glass Nailsea, near Bristol, produced opaque glass with bold decorative streaks from late 18thC. Now any such glass is commonly called "Nailsea".

Newcastle baluster Type of balustroid glass, associated with Tyneside, mid-18thC. Features are more than one knop and a conical bowl.

ogee bowl Bowl of drinking glass with a profile of S-shape.

opaque twist Twist or spiral created in the stem of a glass by laying in a strand of milk or coloured glass; found in especially English glasses of third quarter of 18thC.

pedestal-stem Glass with thick stem narrowing towards the bottom, usually fluted. Early and mid 18thC.

pontil Rod with which the glass is removed from the blowpipe.

pontil mark Mark left when the pontil rod is snapped off, e.g. on the bottom of a glass. *See page 82.*

Glossary

Portland vase An ancient Roman cameo vase, in London's British Museum, that inspired many 19thC cameo artists.

pot The stone bowl that glass is melted in in the furnace.

prunt Blob of glass applied for decoration to the glass body.

ratafia glass 18thC glass used for drinking the liqueur ratafia. Resembles an ale-glass, but is even more slender, the stem merging into the profile of the bowl.

roemer (rummer) Type of goblet, usually with prunts on the thick stem. Often in green ("Waldglas"); made in Bohemia from c1500.

ruby glass Glass containing gold or copper, which makes it red. Technique, perfected in late 17thC in Germany, associated with Bohemia.

St Louis glass Glass made at St Louis in Lorraine, France, from the late 1 8thC; it is famous for coloured glass and paperweights.

step-cut Cut in a series of layers or steps, e.g. the foot of a bowl or drinking glass.

tazza Italian for cup or basin: specifically, a type of glass with a wide bowl, tall stem and spreading foot, made in Venice from late 15thC.

tear Air-bubble in the glass (usually in the stem of a drinking glass) in the shape of a tear-drop. Technique developed in England in early 18thC; from it the air-twist evolved.

terraced Descending in layers, eg an outspreading foot on a drinking glass.

turnover With a rim that turns over, as a cuff does.

twist *See air-, opaque, etc.*

verre de soie From the French for silk glass, glass with a silky finish.

Introduction

FURNITURE

- In the UK oak was the principal material for all furniture up to c1670 and well into the 19thC for country furniture.
- Early oak has patina. Its original golden honey colour ages to a warm chestnut to black, with a rich patination. Stripping and refurbishing destroys colour and sheen, and devalues a piece.
- Wear consistent with use is inevitable, but be aware that restoration can be expensive.
- Avoid pieces which have been "embellished" later. 19thC carving will be in relief with sharp edges.

An English William & Mary oak and pine chest of drawers.

A 17thC oak drop leaf refectory table in the Flemish taste.

Later veneering and inlay is thin, machine-cut, or distinguished by insensitive treatment of grain or anachronistic patterns.
- Rarity is not a guarantee of value. Best prices are paid for exceptional condition, even for a relatively common piece.
- Tables can be dated with

some accuracy by their legs and stretchers. Earliest are simple and square; lathe turning was mastered c1640. 18thC turning restrained and architectural. Later pieces often have heavy bulbous mouldings or over elaborate imitations of earlier styles.
- Period chests in solid, well-worn oak with good decoration, are desirable.
- Chests with drawers and original decoration fetch best prices. Plain board chests are comparatively inexpensive.
- Early oak chests of drawers usually have four flights of drawers, drawers on bottom runners, and plain block or bun feet. Decoration is fielded or coffered panels, with mouldings to disguise joints.
- Check mouldings carefully for brass pins – usually a sign that a piece is 19thC or that mouldings were added later.

Oak and Walnut

- The best dressers are 17thC and 18thC, made for the parlour and elegantly proportioned. By 19thC dressers tended to be relegated to the kitchen, and were constructed of pine.
- In the 19thC mass producers used poorly-seasoned oak which has split and looks old to an inexperienced eye. Check for black lines in the grain, saw marks on hidden edges, thin timbers and machine carving.

A George II oak dresser, the plate rack with dentil cornice.

WALNUT

- Walnut imported from France and Spain became the principal material for furniture in the UK from c1670 until c1730 when France prohibited further walnut exports.
- The period coincides with Restoration of Charles II in England and a new taste for continental flamboyance.
- Walnut lent itself to the new taste because of its rich golden brown colour, with darker brown figuring, and its suitability for veneer work.
- Walnut is easily carved. Characteristically, early walnut pieces have twist turned legs and stretchers and detailed mouldings.
- English furniture joints were mortised and tenon pegged and dowelled. Continental furniture is often simply pegged and legs have stretchers for stability.
- Walnut is especially prone to woodworm and splits easily.
- Do not confuse early walnut with "black" or Virginia walnut. Some later 17thC/early 18thC pieces were made in the latter, but it was mostly used in quantity from 1830.

Drawers

Coming into general use in the early 17thC, the drawer has become an important factor in dating and authenticating furniture. However, remember that dates are always approximate and that rules invariably have exceptions.

Beware

- If handles have been moved or changed: drawer may have been reduced in width. Check reverse of front for filled holes. If no corresponding holes on front, veneer probably later than drawer.

- If the dovetailing in all drawers does not match.

- If dovetails at back of drawer has been altered: drawer depth has been reduced.

- If carcase is not same age as base and back of drawer.

DRAWERS

17th Century drawers

- Early 17thC drawers were nailed together; side runners fitted deep side grooves. Bottom runners from c1680.
- If handles are original surrounding wood will be darker with slight indentations.
- Linings of white or red pine indicate Continental origin.

18th Century drawers

- Drawer linings oak until mid-18thC. Good quality drawers had oak sides.
- Bottom boards made from 2 or 3 pieces of same wood, and grooved to form bottom runners. To c1770 grain in bottom boards ran from front to back; after c1770 from side to side.
- No 18thC drawer exactly fitted space between front and back, a space always being left for ventilation.

19th Century drawers

- Corner mouldings introduced by Sheraton, so indicate a date after 1799.

- Bottom boards made from one piece of wood, usually screwed to sides.
- Machine-made dovetails indicate the piece was made after the 1880s.

Veneers & Marquetry

Veneering is the term used for applying thin sheets of quality wood to a piece of furniture made from a coarser wood. Marquetry involves inlaying designs in wood, using wood of other colours or graining, or other materials.

Beware

- Hand-cut veneers show saw marks when viewed from above; a machine-cut veneer appears much smoother.
- 19thC machine-cut veneers are wafer thin and almost lacking in "figure".

- Veneers occasionally "bubble"; if this bubble can easily be pressed in with the finger, it is either machine-cut, or the surface has been sanded down, probably to obliterate signs of damage.

VENEERS AND MARQUETRY

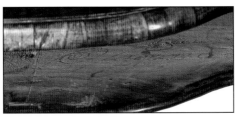

- Veneering has been used since the early 18thC. The earliest veneers were walnut, followed by the superbly patterned mahogany veneers of the late 18thC and early 19thC. Note, however, that walnut returned to favour in the Victorian period. Many other woods were also used as veneers, notably satinwood, rosewood and maple.
- Feather-banding on drawers should be continuous.
- Marquetry began in Europe and was particularly popular in Holland from the end of the 17thC. In England it flourished in the late 18thC, with intricate detail engraved rather than cut as on the Continent.
- Marquetry on walnut fetches more than marquetry on mahogany; and the latter more than marquetry on oak.
- Particularly desirable is marquetry which includes bone and/or mother-of-pearl. Birds and insects are rarer than flowers.
- A vast number of pieces have been re-veneered at some time. This significantly reduces value, so be sure to check.

Repairs, Alterations, Restoration & Marriages

With furniture, pieces are all too often not what they seem at first sight. This is not surprising since wood, by its very nature, is subject to wear, tear and time, is easily damaged, yet responds to careful doctoring. Few pieces of antique furniture escape the need for some form of repair. Such repairs can often be crude, unskilled and of considerable age. However, they need not affect the value to any great extent. Alterations were often made with no dishonest intent, but to conform with changing fashion, personal needs or taste, or to fit available space. For example, in the mid 19thC large Tudor pieces were cut down to fit the Victorian parlour or dining room.

REPAIRS, RESTORATION, ALTERATIONS, MARRIAGES

- Careful repairs by a restorer can produce a piece that is near its original condition. If this restoration is pointed out, such repair is acceptable.
- Other recognized repairs include the removal of French polish applied later, or the stripping of any paint not on the original.
- Structural alterations include tallboys split up to make two chests, with a top added to the base piece and feet to the top.
- A "marriage" is the union of two separate pieces (eg writing bureau and bookcase) to produce a more saleable two-part piece (eg bureau-bookcase). There is no objection to this if the pieces are of the same period and the result is sold as a marriage – though this should be reflected in a lower price.

- Check that carcase wood, veneer, colour, proportions and general "feel" match.
- Marriages are usually evident when viewed from the back, so check the backboards match.

Copies & Fakes

Much 18thC furniture was copied in the 19thC and 20thC. Good examples are not easy to detect, particularly as they have "aged" naturally. Most, however, lack the form and style of the originals. "Reproductions" should be copies of earlier styles made with no intention to deceive. Those made in the second quarter of the 19thC are now sought after.

SPOTTING A FAKE

- Faking is the construction of a piece of furniture so that in all respects it resembles the original piece it fraudulently claims to be.
- Is the wood correct for the piece? Check drawers and backs. The edges of timbers at the back should be black.
- Is the veneer hand-cut? Thin machine-cut veneers are an instant give-away, but are frequently used.
- Are the handles, escutcheons, locks, screws, hinges and casters right? Have been attached to the piece for the whole of its life?
- 18thC brass had a "softer" feel and more subtle colour.
- Is the wear on stretchers, rails, doors, etc., convincing?
- Are the proportions and decoration right for the period? In fakes they are often wrong.
- Some pieces are not outright fakes, originally genuine pieces that have been rebuilt to look like other more desirable items.

These are known as "pastiches". They retain much of their original carcase, and appear genuine at first sight.

- Large pieces of furniture are frequently "cut down" to make smaller, more saleable items.
- Carving is a common subject for the faker. If original, it should always stand "proud" of the piece.

Beds

- The four poster, either with a full canopy over it (tester) and rails for bed curtains, or with a canopy over the head only (half-tester), was most common form until 19thC.
- Very few have survived in original state. From the 1850s, old beds were rebuilt because room sizes had changed and people were taller.
- A skilfully lengthened or widened bed can fetch more than a short and narrow one in original condition.

An early 19thC mahogany cradle, lined with silk.

A Federal mahogany canopy bed, possibly Salem, MA. c1820

- Beds with original drapes are rare. Replacement drapes are costly.
- Early US beds are larger and less likely to have been rebuilt. Good examples are rare.

Cradles

- Any repair or alteration will lower value as many have survived in original condition. Cradle rockers are susceptible to wear; check they have not been removed or replaced.

Daybeds

- Early versions reflect contemporary chair styles. Later, under French Empire influence, they became increasingly elaborate.

Brass beds

- Good quality and usable beds are now very saleable. Original examples are sought after.

A 19thC Anglo-Indian ebonised rosewood four-poster bed. c1820

Bookcases

A George III mahogany secretary bookcase. c1770

Bureau- or secretaire bookcases

- ▣ The evolution of the bookcase or cabinet standing on a bureau or secretaire base began late 17thC and early 18thC.
- ▣ Mahogany pieces should have good colour, patination, mouldings and "fitted" interiors, with original feet and brasses.

A Regency mahogany breakfront secretaire bookcase.

- ▣ Freestanding bookcases introduced in 17thC and perfected in 18thC. The small (dwarf) bookcase without doors became fashionable in late 18thC.
- ▣ 19thC copies usually shorter and Virginia walnut, not mahogany.

An 18thC German or Austrian walnut bureau bookcase.

- ▣ A bureau bookcase should have 3 separate components: bureau base, bookcase and pediment. Veneers should match.
- ▣ On secretaire bookcases an original interior and secret drawers add considerably to value.
- ▣ Many "breakfront bookcases" on the market started life as ordinary 19thC breakfront wardrobes. Look for signs of up to 8in (20cm) having been cut off the depth, and check glazing in frames.

Bureaux

- Bureaux first made in the 1680s of oak, usually in two parts, each with carrying handles, join covered by moulding.
- Most had bun feet, but the originals rarely survive.
- From early 18thC, more common in solid walnut or walnut veneer, often with marquetry or inlay.
- Bracket feet are common from 1710, with an apron from 1720.
- Mahogany was introduced c1720 and became the norm from c1750.
- Continental bureaux of 18th/19thC are often more elaborate in shape and decoration than British ones. French tambour fronted cylinder bureau popular from late 18thC.
- Size is critical to value. Bureaux fetch considerably more if under 38in (96.5cm) in width; 36in (91.5cm) is the ideal size.

A 19thC French Empire style mahogany bureau à cylindre.

- Stepped interiors with a central cupboard, fitted well with cover slide, secret drawers and oak linings add to value.
- Bureaux may be reduced in width to try to increase their value.

A late 19thC Indiana 'extra grade' Wooton desk.

- Avoid any bureau with cracks and splits or replaced flaps.

Bureau cabinets

- Prone to marriage or separation. A bureau intended to bear a cabinet will normally have a steeper fall than one intended to stand alone.

A George II walnut bureau, herringbone banded top. c1740

Desks

Kneehole

- Kneehole desks are the earliest form of desk and date from the early 18thC.
- Usually three drawers across top, three down each pedestal with recessed cupboard between the pedestals.

A George III mahogany twin pedestal desk.

A George II feather-banded walnut kneehole desk.

Davenport

- Small desk derived from design ordered by Captain Davenport in late 1790s. Popular in 19thC. Do not confuse with US sofa.

A Regency Andaman padouk and ebonised davenport.

- Fine veneers, crisp carving, brass stringing, fittings such as concealed drawers add value.

Pedestal

- Made from c1765 onwards. Earliest are larger and more ornate, with all-over dark veneer.
- Built in three pieces, susceptible to marriage.
- When the fashion was for smaller desks, early ones were cut down.

A mahogany Carlton House writing table, c.1800

Carlton House

- First made late 18thC for Prince of Wales' house in Carlton House Terrace, London.
- Embellishment is in the veneer, inlay and mounts, though some later designs have turned legs.
- Beware: Any desk that is not rock solid is likely to be a marriage or of second rate workmanship.

Tables

Refectory table

- Oak refectory table was only type until gateleg and side tables in early 17thC.
- Original pieces are one or two planks wide.

A Charles II oak refectory table.

Gate leg table

- Very early versions have square legs. Turning comes in 1640–1660. Flaps are frequently replaced.

A late 17thC/early 18thC oak gateleg dining table.

Lowboy

- Rarely copied, but check drawers are original. Best prices for cabriole legs.

An early 18thC George I walnut lowboy.

Drop-leaf table

- Came in with widespread use of mahogany c1750. Early walnut examples valuable if in good condition.
- Circular tables superseded by square c1740 and now more valuable. A rectangular leaf cut to oval will lack patina on underside.

A George II mahogany drop leaf dining table. c1750

Card table

- Commonest 18thC form: fold-over top supported on hinged back leg. Better version: legs hinge to open

A Louis XVI style mahogany fold-over games table. c1880

at 45 degrees from frame. Best: late 18thC concertina action. Later version: swivel top on central column.
- Matching pairs are very valuable; look for similar patination on underframe.

Tables

A George III mahogany three-pedestal dining table. c1800

Dining table

- Large, multi-pedestal tables with free-standing D-ends common in 18thC and 19thC, but broken up as unfashionable in 20thC.
- Look for original square legs; later turned legs are less valuable.
- Disguised screwholes, unmatched timbers, new fixings suggest alterations.

A George II mahogany tea table. c1760

Tilt-top table

- Usually rectangular with rounded corners.
- Oval and circular rarer. If oval top added to a period base proportions affected.
- Tops intricately inlaid from c1830.

Pembroke table

- Early square-legged better than later turned and reeded. Rounded flaps more desirable than square; satinwood and marquetry increase value.

A Regency mahogany Pembroke table

Sofa table

- Rosewood especially desirable, as are end supports carved with lyres or Egyptian heads.
- Drawers should be shallow but long drawers better than those later cut down.
- Beware: commonest form of "improvement" is cutting a round or oval top from a square table. Always check that underside patination is continuous. There should be 2in (5cm) minimum overhang between legs and outer edge.

A Regency mahogany sofa table. c1820

Chairs

FURNITURE

A 17thC Dutch walnut Baroque armchair.

A George II Irish mahogany open armchair.

A Regency mahogany dining chair and carver.

- Copying so widespread in 19thC that care is needed to identify genuine early chairs. Look for wear to feet, back and seat.
- The earlier a set of chairs and the more pieces in it, the greater the value; especially if set includes a carver or two. Carver seat should be at least 2in (5cm) wider. Use these ratios to assess the value of sets of average quality compared with single chair price:

    A Pair: 3 times
    Set of 4: 6–7 times
    Set of 6: 10–12 times
    Set of 8: 15 plus times

Armchairs

- To mid 17thC chairs were square, with carved oak panel backs. After 1660, easily carved walnut principal material. Elaborately carved chairs valuable.
- Introduction of cabriole leg c1710, and widespread use of mahogany after 1730 resulted in lighter, stronger chairs. The back splat fits into a shoe which is separate from the back seat rail. If shoe and rail are one, chair is copy.

Dining Chairs

- In last half of 18thC chairs became lighter, simpler and cheaper to make.
- Back splats fit into shoe piece separate from seat frame. Integral shoe piece and seat frame indicates post 1830 date.

FURNITURE

A Regency mahogany and leather tub armchair.

Side, hall and corner chairs

- Decorative chairs often painted, ebonized, gilded and/or inlaid. Though early chairs are usually delicate, legs often plain.
- 19thC copies popular for boudoirs and drawing rooms, increasingly ostentatious and in mahogany rather than earlier beech, birch or satinwood. Many are good, but plain legs tend to be more popular than decorative.

A 19thC Black Forest carved walnut hall chair.

Fancy chairs

- In America, late 18thC/ early 19thC Hepplewhite and Sheraton style chairs were often hand-painted by their owners. Good original

A pair of Pennsylvania fancy side chairs. c1840

pieces are much in demand.

Windsor chairs

- In continuous production since 1720s; good hand-made pieces in demand.
- Clues to dating: cabriole legs 1740–70,

A Philadelphia comb-back Windsor armchair. c1770

wheel splat after 1790, gothic splat and pointed arch back 1760 –1800, bulbous turning post 1830.

Cabinets & Sideboards

Side cabinets/credenzas

■ A "credenza" usually means an ornate Italianate or French-style piece.

A 19thC burr walnut breakfront credenza.

■ The quality of craftsmanship can be surprisingly poor. Be particularly careful with serpentine-fronted pieces with shaped sides.

■ Regency cabinets are desirable and many Victorian mass-produced chiffonniers have been made to look like earlier pieces by

A 19thC Napoleon III side cabinet with hardstone inlay.

the addition of gilt mounts, brass grilles and pleated silk fronts.

■ Damaged tops were sometimes replaced in marble; the value of the resulting piece will depend on the quality and attractiveness of the marble.

Sideboards

■ Dining room furniture, popularized by Robert Adam from c1770. Pieces usually with six square tapering legs. Turned legs are either very early or, more likely, Victorian.

A Gustav Stickley Arts & Crafts sideboard no. 814 1/2.

■ Central drawer should be baize-lined with compartments. Side drawers or cupboards should have containers, racks or cellarets intact. Removal reduces value.

■ Top should be of one piece of timber; two-or three-piece tops are Victorian.

■ US Arts & Crafts pieces are highly desirable. Original finish and hand-wrought iron metalware increases value.

Cabinets

■ Cabinets designed to be ornamental, and to display the owner's prized pieces.

Cabinets & Sideboards

■ Original condition, elaborate interiors, and quality of decoration all add value.

A late George III mahogany and tulipwood sideboard.

■ Glazed display cabinets are more popular than solid or blind doors.

■ Early pieces have small rectangular panes and astragal mouldings. By c1750, crown glass enabled more elaborate shapes. With finely detailed mahogany glazing bars.

■ Cabinets from the Art Nouveau period are desirable, particulary with good marquetry.

■ Cabinets were commonly made from wardrobes in the early 20thC. Look for drawers not cupboards, low base in proportion to top, modern glass and, often, adjustable shelving on "ladders".

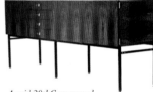

A mid 20thC rosewood sideboard by Alain Richard.

20thC Cabinets & Sideboards

Great demand now for furniture from the 20thC.

■ Particularly popular are pieces by Art Deco designers; Jacques E. Ruhlmann, Jules Leleu, Paul Follot, Paul Frankl and Gilbert Rohde.

■ French designers influenced by new approach to classicism, US designers by skyscraper architechture and Bauhaus.

■ Design is paramount – look for strong lines and exotic materials.

■ Mid-Century Modern also "hot".

An Emile Gallé Art Nouveau mahogany display cabinet.

Cupboards

FURNITURE

Court cupboards

- Date from 16thC. Even skilful repair affects value. Timbers should have same colour, patination.

An Elizabethan oak court cupboard.

- Plain planks at the back should be fixed to the frame with clout nails and show signs of shrinking.

Corner cupboards

- Genuine early pieces should have serpentine or elegantly curving shelves. Those fitted with two or three small drawers are especially desirable.
- Bow fronted pieces fetch

A painted and decorated corner cupboard, Provincetown, MA.

more than commoner flat fronted.

- Folk decorated pieces with original paint are at a premium.
- Few early walnut pieces were glazed. Unless the glazing is Vauxhall mirror glass, suspect that original front has been replaced.

A two-part New Jersey Federal linen press. c1800

Clothes presses

- Typically a low chest with a cupboard above containing shelves, trays on runners or trays and a hanging space.
- Many Regency presses were gutted to make wardrobes; a mid 19thC invention. Best prices are paid for those which still retain good quality oak fittings.

Cupboards

- Most cupboards date from 18thC or later.
- They were functional and more liable to wear and

Cupboards

A Pennsylvania painted pine schrank. c1770

door type. This happened with new furniture and with older pieces which were thus "improved".

Dressers

- Country furniture of oak, ash or elm until mid 19thC when most were made in pine. Early pieces with a decorative canopy or frieze and turned legs, or Arts and Crafts examples, are sought after.
- The majority of those on the market have been repaired. Check timbers have consistent colour, patination and hardness.
- American step-back cupboards are usually two-part pieces and subject to

damage than other furniture, consequently most pieces have been repaired or modified.

- Original untouched pieces in good condition are rare and valuable, particularly those of fruitwood.
- As the 18thC progressed, the use of glass in the manufacture of cabinet furniture became more common, with glazed doors replacing the blind-

A late 18thC American painted pine stepback cupboard.

A mid-18thC French carved oak dresser.

marriage. Check to see that timber and construction match up in both parts.

- Beware: Look at all cupboards with great care. Repair, modification and even marriages may be acceptable but should be reflected in a lower price.

Canterburies, Commodes & Chests

*A 19thC
Classical mahogany canterbury.*

Canterburies

- The first canterburies were made c1700, originally as plate-holders to stand by the supper table.
- The earliest are of mahogany but satinwood examples are known.
- The number of divisions varies, though four is common. Tops are square or slighly convex with a drawer below.

*An Italian walnut and
marquetry commode. c1780*

Commodes

- A chest of drawers in the French style, fashionable from mid 18thC, but never made in quantity because the elaborate shapes and decorative detail were expensive to achieve.

- Serpentine and bombé shapes are the commonest, but rectangular, demi-lune and kettle shapes also found. Secretaire commode with a fall front disguised as top drawer, and fitted interior is rare.
- Commodes are highly decorative, but flamboyance is not a guarantee of value. Decoration must

A late 18thC Louis XVI rose-wood and parquetry commode.

feel integral to the piece, helping to articulate the shape and outlines, not merely applied.
- Later copies of early pieces tend to be scaled down in size to suit smaller rooms.
- Prudery in the 19thC caused any piece of furniture designed to conceal a chamber pot to be called a commode.

Chests

- Coffers with hinged lids used from 13thC to early 18thC; copied in 19thC.
- Chests fitted entirely with drawers date from mid 17thC.

Coffers

- Pre-Jacobean coffers rare; 17thC examples survive,

Canterburies, Commodes & Chests

A Charles II and later panelled oak coffer.

19thC copies common.
■ Early examples will never show saw marks; splintering along the grain will have been worn smooth.

Mule Chest
■ The Mule chest, with drawer beneath coffer,

A late 18thC Pennsylvania painted dower chest.

introduced end 16thC.
■ 18th and 19thC US painted dower chests with original paint are valuable. Many were repainted later.

A late 17thC oak mule chest, with profuse carving.

Chests of drawers
■ Drawers are particularly diagnostic in recognizing the best pieces. Up to c1660 drawers ran on side bearers, afterwards on bottom runners.

A late 17thC William & Mary oak chest of drawers.

■ 18thC drawers never run the full depth of the chest. Drawers without locks will be 19thC or later.
■ Walnut pieces and serpentine shapes, more likely to be original since they were

A George III mahogany serpentine chest of drawers. c1770

expensive to produce.
■ Late 17thC and 18thC examples generally less heavy in construction.
■ 19thC saw increase in size and decrease in quality in attempt to satisfy demand.

Wine Coolers, Dumb Waiters, Mirrors & Stools

*A George III
mahogany three-tier dumb waiter.*

Dumb waiters

- Produced in 1720s but not in quantity until 1750s.
- Earliest generally of three tiers, though two tier examples are found.
- Early examples are usually made from mahogany.

An 18thC-style gilt-wood and gesso over-mantel mirror.

Mirrors

- Until 1773 looking glass was blown from cylinders of glass, which limited the size. So, early mirrors are

either small, or made of 2 or 3 pieces covered by astragal bars at the join.

- The reflective image in old glass is dark. When viewed at an angle it

A giltwood convex mirror, with eagle pediment. c1800

appears grey in tone.

- Until the 19thC, frames usually wood covered with gilt gesso or carved giltwood. 19thC frames tended to be stucco.
- Candle arms on pier glasses and sconces on cheval mirrors add value.

A mid-17thC oak joint stool, on baluster turned legs. c1660

Wine Coolers, Dumb Waiters, Mirrors & Stools

A George III mahogany framed stool. c1760

Stools

- Apart from benches, stools were main form of seating until late 17thC when chairs took over.
- Signs of an early piece are coarse cut timbers, curving seat of split, not sawn, timber, good overhang, wear to legs, feet and stretchers, all-over polish and patination.
- Finely turned legs and a decorated frieze add to the value.

A carved mahogany and parcel gilt upholstered footstool. c1900

Wine coolers

- Wine coolers, generally of mahogany, were popular from c1730 until the late 19thC.
- Cisterns have open tops, whilst cellarets are fitted with a locking lid.
- There are two main types: those with integral feet or a pedestal which were

A George III mahogany and brass bound wine cooler.

made to stand on a sideboard; and those with legs or a separate stand, made to stand on the floor.

- Coolers of coopered construction are commoner than jointed forms. Round, oval hexagonal and octagonal shapes are all found in coopered form with an upper and a lower brass ring.

- Hessian under an upholstered seat indicates post 1840 date or conceal alterations to an earlier piece.

A late Regency mahogany sarcophagus-shaped cellaret.

How to identify woods

FURNITURE

Amboyna

Beech

Birch

Birch

Calamander

Cherry

Chestnut

Coromandel

How to identify woods

Ebony

Elm

Elm (burr)

Flame Mahogony

Kingwood

Mahogony

Mahogony (II)

Maple

How to identify woods

FURNTIURE

Maple, Bird's Eye

Oak (Dark)

Oak (Light)

Olive

Pine

Pine

Rosewood

Rosewood

How to identify woods

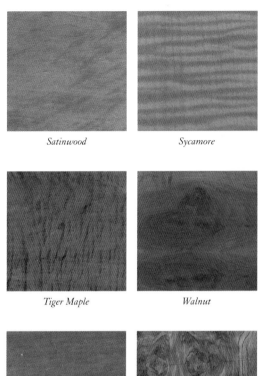

Satinwood

Sycamore

Tiger Maple

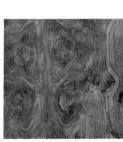

Walnut

Walnut

Walnut (burr)

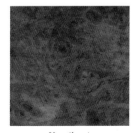

Yew (burr)

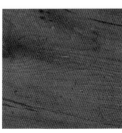

Yew

Chair Backs

FURNITURE

Country Styles

Early 18thC banister, US

Mid 18thC ladderback, US

Late 18thC Windsor comb-back, US

Late 19thC Windsor braceback, US

Mid 19thC Windsor hoop spindle, UK

Polite Styles

Early 17thC carved pierced crested rails, Spain

Early 17thC ball, baluster, ring turned back, England

17thC yoke-back with protruding top rail, China

Mid 17thC carved and pierced top rail, England

Mid 17thC arched and carved top rail, England

Late 17thC lobed and scroll carved arched crest, England

Early 18thC Queen Anne solid vasiform splat, Ireland

Chair backs

Early 18thC George I shaped vasiform backrest, UK

Early 18thC Queen Anne scalloped crest and padded back, US

Early 18thC shaped splat, and carved top rail, UK

Mid 18thC Louis XV with shaped back rail, France

Mid 18thC cupid's bow crest over a vasiform splat, US

Mid 18thC Louis XV rococo giltwood cartouche, France

Mid 18thC George III simulated bamboo cock-pen, UK

Late 18thC pierced splat with leaf-scroll carving, US

Late 18thC George III pierced ladderback, UK

Late 18thC shield-shaped with painted pierced splat, UK

Late 18thC open lattice-work back, with central panel, China

Late 18thC arched top rail, pierced and waisted splay, UK

Chair Backs

Late 18thC Louis XVI giltwood frame upholstered, France

Late 18thC Louis XVI giltwood oval upholstered, France

Early 19thC Federal carved and inlaid shield-back, US

Early 19thC wide curved crest rail with lattice splats, France

Early 19thC Empire curved backrest with a lyre form splat, US

Early 19thC George III vertical back slats, UK

Early 19thC Regency with pierced bar splat, UK

Early 19thC Regency lyre-shaped back, UK

Early 19thC with a over an S-scroll pierced back, UK

Early 19thC with a leaf carved horizontal splat, UK

Early 19thC with carved and pierced splat, Germany

Early 19thC classical scrolled crest and urn-form splat, US

Chair Backs

Early 19thC central splat, with Neo-classical emblems, France

Early 19thC curved and carved top rail and splats, Germany

Early 19thC over-scrolled top rail with arched back, UK

Early 19thC Gothic crest rail, carved capitols on supports, US

Early 19thC Empire rectangular frame upholstered, France

Mid 19thC Louis Philippe balloon back, France

Mid 19thC heart-shaped back with armorial shield, UK

Mid 19thC Thonet bentwood scrolling backs, Austria

Mid 19thC Gothic baluster turned padded back, UK

Late 19thC with D-form wings and palmette rails, China

Late 19thC Gothic carved, pierced back, Germany

Late 19thC sheild back with arched crest, UK

Chair Backs

Late 19thC cut with stylized cloverleaf reticulation, US

Late 19thC Arts and Crafts painted panelled back, UK

Late 19thC mihrab-arched bobbin work back, Syria

Late 19thC arched top rail with tall caned splat, UK

Early 20thC Art Nouveau assymetrical pierced, Italy

Early 20thC Art Nouveau shaped and pierced back, UK

Early 20thC Art Nouveau roundel, Italy

Early 20thC Art Nouveau pierced floral carving, France

Early 20thC Arts and Crafts vertical slats and corbels, US

Early 20thC Art Nouveau padded with slatted gallery, UK

Early 20thC solid oak supported on columns, US

Early 20thC Art Nouveau carved central splat, UK

Chair Backs

Early 20thC Arts & Crafts vertical back splats, US

Early 20thC Arts & Crafts ladderback, UK

1930s Pine 'zig-zag', The Netherlands

Early 20thC Art Nouveau with pierced back, France

Art Deco banded fan-back, France

1930s steel with leather strapping, US

Post-1958 Verner Panton's wire cone, Denmark

1960s Pedro Freideberg's 'Left Hand Fingers', Mexico

1968 George Nakashima's hickory back spindles, US

1986 Philippe Starck's leather over steel frame, France

1984 Robert Venturi's 'Queen Anne' splat, US

1990 Philippe Starck's 'W-W'-stool, France

Legs

FURNITURE

Late 17thC block and turned leg, UK

Late 17thC carved scrolling leg, UK

Early 18thC bobbin turned leg, UK

Late 17thC cup and turned leg, Holland

Late 17thC baluster turned leg, UK

Early 18thC square and baluster, UK

Early 18thC Queen Anne turned leg, UK

Early 18thC carved cabriole leg, France

Early 18thC inverted trumpet turned leg, US

Early 18thC trumpet turned leg, US

Early 18thC shell carved cabriole leg, UK

Early 18thC George II c-scroll leg, UK

Early 18thC leaf-carved cabriole leg, UK

Late 18thC turned leg, US

Late 18thC cabriole leg, snake foot, US

Late 18thC square tapering leg, UK

Legs

Late 18thC scroll cabriole leg, UK

Late 18thC Chippendale cabriole leg, US

Late 18thC carved cabriole leg, US

Late 18thC tapering leaf-motif leg, Italy

Late 18thC outward-scrolled leg, UK

Late 18thC turned leg, France

Late 18thC square tapering leg, UK

Early 19thC square tapering leg, France

Early 19thC Regency reeded sabre leg, UK

Early 19thC turned leg, France

Early 19thC reeded tapering leg, UK

Early 19thC Grecian turned, reeded leg, UK

Early 19thC Regency ring turned leg, UK

Early 19thC round lobed leg, France

Early 19thC fluted turned tapered leg, UK

Early 19thC Regency sabre leg, UK

Legs

FURNITURE

Early 19thC reeded, tapered leg, France

Early 19thC reeded sabre leg, UK

Early 19thC reeded turned tapering leg, UK

Early 19thC reeded tapering leg, India

Early 19thC baluster shaped tapering, UK

Early 19thC acanthus-carved leg, UK

Mid 19thC shell-carved sabre leg, Sri Lanka

Mid 19thC ring turned leg, UK

Mid 19thC Gothic turned tapered leg, UK

Late 19thC Renaissance, in-curved leg, UK

Late 19thC carved 'femme fleur' leg, Italy

Early 20thC Arts & Crafts, US

Early 20thC Arts & Crafts, US

Mid 20thC square section, Holland

Mid 20thC scrolled carved leg, US

Mid 20thC outward scrolled, US

Feet

Early 18thC Spanish front foot and bun back foot, US

Early 18thC William and Mary bold bun foot, US

Early 18thC flattened ball turned foot, US

Mid 18thC Chippendale ball and claw foot, US

Mid 18thC Chippendale ball and claw foot, US

Late 18thC boldly carved ball and claw foot, Holland

Late 17thC William and Mary bracket foot, England

Late 18thC ogee moulded bracket foot, US

Early 19thC splayed bracket foot, UK

Mid 18thC crooked pad foot, US

Mid 18thC Queen Anne pad foot, US

Mid 18thC Chippendale slipper foot, US

Mid 18thC rococo stylised hoof foot, Italy

Early 19thC acanthus and paw foot, US

Early 19thC Regency carved lion paw foot, UK

Early 19thC classical scroll and paw foot, US

Late 19thC Renaissance Revival paw foot, US

Early 19thC Regency scrolled foot, UK

Handles

FURNITURE

Late 17thC brass drop handle, England

Early 18thC brass drop handle, with round backplate, UK

Early 18thC pierced brass drop handle, UK

Mid 18thC ormolu Rococo handle, Sweden

Mid 18thC rococo cast brass handle, UK

Mid 18thC solid brass ring handle, UK

Late 18thC foliate cast brass drop handle, UK

Late 18thC brass backplate and swan-neck handle, US

Early 19thC brass lion mask ring handle, UK

Early 19thC brass oval embossed handle, US

Early 19thC oval brass handle, UK

Early 19thC classical brass pull, US

Early 19thC foliate brass ring handle, UK

Early 20thC Arts & Crafts, US

Early 20thC Arts & Crafts, US

1930s Art Deco bakelite knob, US

1930s Art Deco brass and ebonised pull, US

1940s Art Deco leather strap and gilt ring handle, France

Pediments

Early 17thC dentil moulded and carved pediment, England

Early 18thC pierced railed pediment, Spain

Early 18thC moulded, broken triangular pediment, UK

Early 18thC open arched pediment, UK

Early 18thC Queen Anne double dome pediment, US

Mid 18thC architectural pediment, South German

Mid 18thC arched pediment, centred by a cresting, UK

Mid 18thC broken pediment, pierced with leaf scrolls, UK

Late 18thC broken arch bonnet pediment, UK

Late 18thC double bonnet top, US

Late 18thC arched leaf crested pediment, Holland

Early 19thC arched bonnet pediment, with finial, France

Early 19thC open swan-neck pediment, UK

Early 19thC swan-neck bonnet top, with finials, US

Early 19thC Regency arched pediment, UK

Early 19thC Gothic Revival serpentine ogee arch, US

Mid 19thC Biedermeier arched pediment, Germany

Late 19thC carved pierced lattice-work, UK

AALTO, ALVAR (1898-1976)

Leading Finnish exponent of the modern movement with a strong humanist outlook. Began designing furniture in 1925.

- Favoured an organic, practical approach to design, using wood, particularly natural birch and laminated birch plywood, rather than more modern materials.
- 1933: Patented method of bending wood.
- 1935: Founded Artek to produce his own designs.
- Some marked "Aalto Mobler, Svensk, Kvalitet Sprodurt".
- Most pieces have a metal label with model number.

BELTER, JOHN HENRY (1804-63)

Born in Germany, moved to New York in 1833 and by 1844 was established as one of city's most fashionable and talented furniture makers. Made breakthroughs in wood lamination process.

- Fashioned extremely strong laminate panels by affixing thin strips of wood together. Strength of these panels allowed elaborate piercing, deep naturalistic carving and dramatic curves which characterised his Rococo Revival style.
- After Belter's death his business was continued by his brother-in-law until 1867 with less success.

BREUER, MARCEL (1902-81)

One of the first furniture designers to employ the new material of tubular steel in the 1920s. Breuer's stripped-down modernist designs remain extremely influential.

- Studied at the Weimar Bauhaus, Germany, from 1920, and oversaw the furniture workshop there from 1924-8.
- First tubular steel design, the Wassily Chair, produced in 1925.
- Co-founded Standard-Möbel in 1927 to manufacture his furniture designs.
- Aluminium pieces produced from 1934.
- Moved to London in 1935 and designed plywood furniture for Isokon.
- Later focused on architectural projects.

CHIPPENDALE, THOMAS (1718-79)

One of a number of highly skilled craftsmen working in London in the middle of the 18thC. His elegant furniture designs were hugely influential and 'Chippendale' has become a generic term applied to both furniture made in London between about 1750 and 1765 and to furniture made since in the same style.

- 1749: set up business as a cabinet-maker in London. Following early success, in 1753 he leased large premises in St. Martin's Lane from where he and a team of craftsmen designed and manufactured a wide range of furniture.

- 1754: wrote 'The Gentleman and Cabinet-Maker's Director', intended to cultivate further patronage and also featured instructions to craftsmen who were invited to copy the designs.

- Most famous for his chairs, which typically have a carved and pierced back splat, a serpentine top rail, carved knees, cabriole legs and claw-and-ball feet.

- Drawing on the popularity of chinoiserie, Chippendale produced a large number of designs inspired by traditional Chinese motifs and details.

- The mid to late 18thC revival in Gothic tastes saw Chippendale publish and produce designs including pointed arches, finials and panels with quatrefoil motifs.

- 'American Chippendale': furniture produced in America, mainly in Philadelphia, from c1745 to c1775 by immigrants from Europe and local craftsmen inspired by his designs.

- American Chippendale (below right) is generally less ornate and made mostly from wood, rather than veneers over a secondary wood as in English examples (below left).

Le Corbusier

LE CORBUSIER (1887-1965)

French company Le Corbusier's (Charles-Edouard Jeanneret-Gris) bold, minimalist and industrial-looking furniture epitomized the ideals of the early Modernists.

- Most furniture designed in collaboration with Charlotte Perriand and Pierre Jeanneret.
- First range of furniture designs produced in 1928, including the B306 Chair and 'Gran Confort' chaise longue.
- Utilized newly popularized tubular steel.
- Later career focused more on architectural projects.

EAMES, CHARLES & RAY

American husband and wife Charles (1907-78) and Ray (1912–88) Eames produced work that married industry and art.

- Flexible, affordable, fresh materials: moulded plywood, plastic, fibreglass and aluminium. Inspired by Japanese architecture, Scandinavian design and Modernism.
- From 1947: Collaborate with The Herman Miller Furniture Company.

EASTLAKE, CHARLES LOCKE

English architect (1836-1906) helped shift fashion away from ornate interiors.

- Design philosophy embraced honesty of materials and construction, rectilinear forms and geometric patterns.
- 1868: Published 'Hints on Household Tastes in Furniture, Upholstery and Other Details'.
- 'Eastlake' style more popular in US where it had more decorative form.

ELFE, THOMAS (1719-75)

Elfe was an English-born cabinet- and chairmaker who emigrated to the US and worked in Charleston, South Carolina.

- Produced high quality furniture in Chippendale style.
- Distinctive use of fretwork as a means of decoration.
- Chairs: elaborate formal pieces, examples of decoration and styles include 'carved back', 'fronts fluted', 'compass seated' and 'brass nailed'.
- Much of his work known from his detailed accounts books.

Gillows

FORNASETTI, PIERO (1913-88)

An Italian child prodigy with a talent for painting and drawing.

- 1940: Gio Ponti asked him to produce patterns for his furniture.
- Designs were richly embellished, unlike other Modernist furniture.
- Inspired by Classicism, the Surrealists and illusionism. Many designs used a trompe l'oeil effect.

FRANKL, PAUL (1887-1958)

Born in Vienna, but fled to New York in 1914 to escape WWI. Inspired by Le Corbusier and Walter Gropius.

- 1925: Began producing "Skyscraper" range of custom-made furniture inspired by the New York skyline.
- Made from oak and California redwood; designed to be affordable.

GALLÉ, EMILE (1846-1904)

Gallé was a French Art Nouveau furniture and glass designer. Influenced by the natural world/ history of art/ Symbolist poetry and literature.

- Founded École de Nancy in 1901, based on English Arts & Crafts guild system.
- Furniture made from richly coloured/exotic woods, decorated with organic marquetry designs.

GILLOWS

Firm of cabinetmakers established in Lancaster, UK, c1730.

- 1769: Open London branch.
- Furniture for nobility, gentry and middle classes.
- Mainly Neo-classical designs. Used mahogany or satinwood. Carefully matched figured veneers.
- Furniture often stamped with Gillows name.

FURNITURE

HEAL & SONS

British furniture retailer and manufacturer founded in 1810,
based in Tottenham Court Road, London, from 1818. Renowned
for innovative designs. Known for illustrated catalogues.

- In late 19thC/early 20th C had great success based on range of
  Arts & Crafts furniture. Also made/retailed Art Deco furniture.
- Utilized sycamore, oak or limed oak.
- Marcel Breuer contributed designs during the 1930s.
- Furniture essentially machine-made but finished by hand.
- Company still in existence.

HEPPLEWHITE, GEORGE (1727?-1786)

English craftsman whose pattern book disseminated Neo-classical
design for the mass market.

- 1788: 'Cabinet-Maker and
  Upholsterer's Guide' published
  by his widow. No actual furni-
  ture attributed to him.
- Particular influence on US
  Federal style.

HOFFMANN, JOSEF (1870-1956)

Austrian architect and designer who
created a purer, more linear version of Art
Nouveau that served as link between Art
Nouveau and Modernism.

- Influenced by both Charles Rennie
  Mackintosh and simple classicism of
  Austrian Biedermeier.
- 1903: Co-founded Wiener Werkstätte,
  centre of progressive design in Vienna.
- Designed for Thonet (*see p155*).

INCE, WILLIAM (d.1804)

English cabinet-maker who adopted and helped spread the
Neo-classical style of the 1750s and 1760s.

- 1762: with John Mayhew, published 'The Universal System
  of Household Furniture'. Ince & Mayhew cabinetmakers had
  been established in 1758.
- Ince and Mayhew's book also featured designs inspired by the
  Orient, reflecting and promoting the European interest in
  Chinese and Japanese decorative objects of the period.

Limbert

KOHN, JACOB (1791-1868) & JOSEF (1817-84)

Jacob Kohn and his son Josef became recognised as leading manufacturers of simple, well-designed and well-made furniture aimed at the middle classes.

- 1850: Manufacturing company established in Vienna.
- J.J. Kohn specialized in bentwood furniture, following Michael Thonet's pioneering work with the bentwood technique (*see p155*).
- Early 20thC: Reputation enhanced with manufacture of a number of Josef Hoffmann's designs.

JACOB, GEORGES (1739-1814)

French cabinet-maker of the late 18thC and early 19thC, who produced furniture during reigns of both Louis XVI and Napoleon.

- Inventive designs for chairs, beds, and screens carved with motifs such as twisted ribbons, guilloches, beading, and fluting.
- Pioneer and proponent of the French Empire style.
- Supplied furniture for the Palais des Tuileries.
- Designs also particularly favoured in early 19thC Russia.

JACOBSEN, ARNE (1902-71)

Danish architect and designer. Early career focused on architecture, worked as a furniture designer after 1945.

- Initial designs clearly influenced by Le Corbusier and Gunnar Asplund.
- Individual style apparent in 1950s.
- 1955: 'Series 7' chair designed, an estimated 6 million have been sold.
- Designs still in production.

LIMBERT, CHARLES (1854-1923)

Made Arts & Crafts oak furniture in Grand Rapids, Michigan, US.

- Designs strongly influenced by both Gustav Stickley and Charles Rennie Mackintosh.
- Pieces are typically pale oak and crafted to a high standard.
- Mark: rectangular with a craftsman at work.
- Factory closed in 1944.

Mackintosh, Charles Rennie

FURNITURE

MACKINTOSH, CHARLES RENNIE

Scottish architect (1868-1928) and designer, helped establish 'Glasgow School' style.

- Pioneered confident style of straight lines and gentle curves which contrasted with English Arts & Crafts and influenced Art Nouveau.
- Furniture produced under his own name and for Glasgow furniture makers of Guthrie and Wells.

MAJORELLE, LOUIS (1859-1926)

French furniture designer who worked at Gallé's École de Nancy where he created some of the finest pieces of Art Nouveau furniture.

- Mainly utilized dark hardwoods such as mahogany, rosewood.
- Worked with Daum brothers (*see p94*) to produce lamps.

MORRIS, WILLIAM (1834-96)

English founding father of the Arts and Crafts movement, Morris extolled the virtues of traditional skills over mechanical production to produce simple, well-made objects.

- Established 'Morris, Marshall, Faulkner & Company' in 1861 to provide integrated decorating services.
- 1875: changed company name to 'Morris & Co.' and concentrated on stained glass and furniture.

NAKASHIMA, GEORGE (1905-90)

Produced distinctive and finely crafted wooden furniture.

- Interned in Idaho from 1942-43, due to Japanese ancestry, where he began learning traditional Japanese carpentry.
  - From 1943: made furniture from a small workshop in New Hope, Pennsylvania.
    - Worked mainly on private commissions.

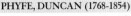

FURNITURE

PHYFE, DUNCAN (1768-1854)

Scottish-born cabinet-maker, moved to New York in 1792 and became one of most prolific craftsmen in US.

- Produced furniture in a series of European styles. Has given his name to generic furniture in the Late Federal and Empire styles.
- Few pieces can be conclusively linked to him.

PONTI, GIO (1891-1979)

Italian architect and designer, worked in many styles and across a range of disciplines, many in collaboration with Piero Fornasetti.

- 1928: 'Domus' magazine launch.
- From 1933: Artistic director of 'Fontana Arte' manufacturer.
- 1946-50: Glass for Venini.
- 1957: 'Superleggera' chair for Cassina.

PROUVÉ, JEAN (1901-84)

French furniture designer with a strong industrial aesthetic who favoured working in metal.

- 1923: Opened first workshop in Nancy. Received commissions from both Le Corbusier and Pierre Jeanneret.

- 1931: Founded Société de Ateliers de Jean Prouvé. Expanded to become Les Ateliers Jean Prouvé in 1947.
- 1954: Set up Paris design studio.

PUGIN, AUGUSTUS WELBY (1812-52)

English architect of French descent and the leading champion of the 19thC Gothic revival.

- Published works extolling 'pure' Gothic style, which fuelled the 19thC interest in this style.
- Provided furnishings for the Houses of Parliament as well as assisting with the design of the building.
- Designed over 100 notable buildings, and produced a wide range of furnishings and decorative iteams including stained glass, ceramics, wrought iron, wallpaper and book illustrations.

FURNITURE

RIESENBURGH, BERNARD VAN (c1700-65)

Dutch-born cabinet-maker who worked in Paris, producing some of the most highly prized work of the Louis XVI period.

■ Rococo designs feature exquisite marquetry and Boulle work.

■ Received a number of commissions for the Palace of Versailles, as well as for foreign clients such as Frederick Augustus II, the Elector of Saxony.

RIESENER, JEAN-HENRI (1734-1806)

German born craftsman who moved to France where he became master ébéniste (cabinet-maker) to Louis XVI.

■ Initially produced very rich and ornate furniture. Adopted a plainer style around 1780.

■ Many of his pieces featured complicated mechanisms that raised or lowered table-tops or angled reading stands.

RIETVELD, GERRIT (1888-1964)

Dutch architect and designer and member of 'De Stijl' group who created a number of classic modern furniture designs.

■ Famous 'Red and Blue' chair created in 1923.

■ Experimented with tubular steel but favoured wood as main material.

ROENTGEN, DAVID (1743-1807)

German cabinet-maker who created Neo-classical furniture of unparalleled quality and innovation.

■ 1768: took over father's furniture workshop. By 1783 had supplied furniture to royal courts of Prussia, France and Russia.

ROHLFS, CHARLES (1853-1936)

A key player in US Arts & Crafts movement who combined Art Nouveau style decoration with clean-lined rectilinear shapes.

■ Produced a range of custom-built furniture from studio in Buffalo, New York.

■ 1899-1900: Exhibition of Gothic-style pieces at Marshall Field department store, Chicago.

ROYCROFT

Community of Arts & Crafts-inspired craftsmen (known as the Roycrofters) founded by Elbert Green Hubbard in East Aurora, New York, 1895.

- Initially produced simple pieces for own community, later expanding output to produce pieces to sell to for visitors.
- Furniture marked with either orb-and-cross symbol (cross with two horizontal bars and an "R" within a circle) or "Roycroft".
- Production ended 1938.

RUHLMANN, ÉMILE-JACQUES (1879-1933)

French furniture designer and craftsman who produced deluxe Art Deco furniture during the 1920s and early 1930s.

- Extravagant display at the 1925 Paris Exhibition established his reputation as a master furniture maker.
- Inspired by classical design elements and craftsmanship ideals found in 18thC furniture. Work typically simple, elegant forms with gentle curves.
- Used rare woods including ebony, rosewood, and amboyna burl, usually in combination and often embellished with ivory.

SHERATON, THOMAS (1751-1806)

English designer and author of practical and influential books on furniture design.

- 'Cabinet-Maker and Upholsterer's Drawing Book' produced between 1791-94
- Two-volume 'The Cabinet Dictionary' published 1803.
- Influential furniture designs gave name to pieces characterized by lightness, elegance and extensive use of inlay.

SOTTSASS, ETTORE (1917-2007)

Italian furniture and product designer and founder of the Memphis group of designers. Has been called the father of Postmodern design.

- 1958: became design director at Italian firm Olivetti, designing office furniture and electronics.
- 1980: founded Memphis group, first exhibition in April 1981 shows group's radical furniture designs.
- Left Memphis in 1985 to concentrate on Sottsass Associati design and architecture group.

Stickley family

FURNITURE (sidebar)

STICKLEY BROTHERS

The Stickleys formed a series of US furniture companies during the late 19thC and early 20thC. The eldest, Gustav, was the most prominent and a figure-head of the US Arts & Crafts movement.

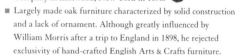

Gustav Stickley (1858-1942)

- Founded the Gustav Stickley Company in Eastwood, New York in 1898.
- Largely made oak furniture characterized by solid construction and a lack of ornament. Although greatly influenced by William Morris after a trip to England in 1898, he rejected exclusivity of hand-crafted English Arts & Crafts furniture.
- 1901: Began to publish a monthly magazine 'The Craftsman' and renamed his business United Crafts. In 1904 he changed the name of his business again to The Craftsman Workshops.

Stickley Brothers and L. & J.G. Stickley

- In 1891 John George Stickley (1871-1921) and his brother Albert (1862-1928) set-up their own furniture company.
- When John left to join his other brother Leopold, Albert continued to run the factory, producing furniture in a more decorative style than any of his brothers' designs.
- In 1904 Leopold Stickley (1869-1957) set up the Onondaga Shops. Later that year he joined his brother John George to establish L. & J.G. Stickley in New York. In 1906 their company was renamed Handcraft and from 1912 was known as The Work of L & J.G. Stickley.
- Leopold and John George utilized mechanical production.
- In 1916 Leopold and John George took over Gustav's The Craftsman Workshops after he ran into financial difficulties.
- The final Stickley company passed out of the family's control in 1974 but is still in operation.

THOMPSON, ROBERT (1876-1955)

English furniture maker from Yorkshire who played an important role in the 1920s craft revival.

- Furniture made largely by hand using traditional techniques, inspired by 17thC designs.
- Became known as the 'Mouseman' because his work is signed with the carved figure of a mouse.

GEBRÜDER THONET

Michael Thonet (1796-1871) invented bentwood technique which involved bending beech strips into curves using steam. Developed in the 1830s.

- 1849 set up Gebrüder Thonet furniture company with his five sons.
- Most famous design model No.14 chair, designed in 1859.
- Company continues today and has collaborated with numerous influential designers.

MIES VAN DER ROHE, LUDWIG (1886-1969)

German architect and designer of major importance to the Modern movement and the International style of architecture.

- Director of the Bauhaus from 1930.
- Designed cantilevered furniture in tubular steel for Berliner Metallgewerbe.
- 'Barcelona' chair (1929) and 'Brno' chair (1930) considered modern classics.

WRIGHT, FRANK LLOYD (1867-1959)

Influential architect and furniture designer, leading figure in US Arts & Crafts and Prairie School movements.

- Founding member of the Chicago Arts and Crafts Society in 1897.
- Interiors and furnishings were integral to the design of his buildings.
- Stressed the importance of machines to produce affordable furniture.

Glossary

apron Decorative skirt of wood set between the legs of a chair or cabinet.

armoire French term for a press, wardrobe or any similarly large cupboard.

associated Not original, but of same period and style. Losses are often made good with "associated" parts.

baluster One of set of upright posts supporting a balustrade. Baluster shapes (eg baluster splat) always have a dominant convex swell at the base terminating in a smaller concave one at the neck.

barley-sugar twist Colloquial name for spiral turned legs and rails, popular from mid 17thC.

block front The front of a piece of furniture shaped from thick boards, so allowing a recessed centre section.

bobbin In the shape of a bobbin or reel: usually a turned element resembling a row of connected spheres.

bombé Outswelling (eg the front of a cabinet which is not flush, but curves forward).

bonheur du jour Small writing table, sometimes with a cupboard above, introduced in France, second half 18thC.

bracket foot The foot itself is plain, but where it is joined to the rail or stretcher it is carved or stepped like an ornamental bracket.

breakfront With a central section that projects or "breaks" forward.

buffet Term for a two-part sideboard.

bun feet Feet shaped like flattened globe. Introduced late 17thC.

burr Deformation to a tree caused eg by the stunted growth of a branch: used in veneer, it gives a decorative pattern or "figure".

cabriole leg Leg, often for a chair, that curves out at the foot and in at the top. The point of change from outer to inner curve is termed the "knee". Introduced in 17thC, the cabriole leg was fundamental to the development of furniture, revolutionizing not only

style, but the way furniture could be constructed.

carcase The inner frame or "chassis" of a piece of furniture, commonly made of an inferior wood and veneered.

cavetto Moulding making an inward curve across a right angle.

chamfer An angle that has been bevelled or flattened off, eg an octagon is a chamfered square. A "sunk" or "hollow" chamfer has a trough or groove in it.

chauffeuse Low fireside chair.

chiffonnier A low or side cupboard. Original 18thC pieces had solid doors replaced in 19thC with lattice or glass doors.

cornice The horizontal top part or cresting of a piece of furniture.

cross-banding Decorative edging, in which the veneer is cross-grained.

davenport In Britain a small writing desk, usually with drawers at side; in the US a bed-couch or sofa.

dentil Small moulding in the shape of a block or tooth, usually found under a cornice. Properly an element of the Corinthian Order.

deudarn Welsh name for two-tier press or hall cupboard.

ebonize To stain a light-coloured wood to the colour of ebony.

escritoire Cabinet with a fall front which lowers to form a writing surface.

fauteuil Upholstered armchair with open sides and padded

elbows. Popular in Britain and America in mid 19thC.

fielded With a raised central area or "field", usually set off by a frame or surround, eg fielded panel.

figure The pattern made by the natural grain through a wood.

frieze Any long ornamental strip.

Glossary

FURNITURE

gadroon Type of carved edge decoration or moulding, consisting of a series of grooves or "flutes" ending in a curved lip, with a ridge between them.

girandole Shaped wall mirror in carved gilt frame with candle branches.

herringbone banding Decorative edging, in which the veneer is laid down in a series of oblique stripes.

inlay The setting of one material (eg marble, wood, metal, tortoiseshell, mother-of-pearl) in or over another. Inlay techniques include marquetry.

marquetry The use of veneer

and often other inlays to make decorative patterns.

moulding Decorative shaped band eg around a panel.

mount Fitting mounted on or attached to furniture, almost invariably of metal, sometimes ormolu.

ogee (ogive) Any S-curve shape. An ogee arch is composed of two meeting S-curves.

ormolu Any mount, sconce or article, that is gilt or at least gold-coloured. "Ormoulu" is French for "powdered gold".

ovolo Moulding making an outward curve across a right angle.

oyster veneer Veneer with a concentric grain resembling an open oyster-shell. Achieved by making a

slanting cut across the grain of a branch.

pediment The equivalent in classical architecture of a gable: a triangular head or topping. A "broken" pediment has the apex of the triangle removed.

rail A horizontal member, running berween the legs or outer uprights of a piece.

scroll Any membrane (eg paper) that has been rolled up. In practice, the shape meant is usually that of a curling tongue. Chair legs or backs often carved with a relief scroll at foot or top.

spindle In the shape of a spinner's spindle. Specifically the upright bars of a spindle-back chair.

splat The central upright of a chair back. This may take

various decorative shapes (eg baluster splat) and may be plain, carved, pierced or inlaid (eg marquetry). Loosley applied to all members in a chair back.

squab cushion Detachable or loose flat cushion for a bench or seat.

S-scroll Decorative Classical ornament in the shape of an 'S', can be carved or applied, developed during the Rococo period.

stiff-leaf toe cap A caster moulded with formalized leaves.

stile Old name for an upright on a chair back, usually associated with early furniture.

stile foot A plain and square-cut foot.

strapwork In furniture, ornament in the form of a

scrolling pattern of bands and straps, 16thC, 17thC and revived.

streamlined Term used to describe US Art Deco

furniture with smooth, clean-lined shapes.

stretcher The rail joining and stabilizing the legs of a chair or table.

turnery Anything "turned" on a lathe and so cut with a circular form of decoration.

veneer Thin sheet or band of wood laid over another (the carcase) as part of a marquetry pattern, or simply for its decorative grain, colour and figure.

wainscot Quarter-cut oak of any kind, but usually in panels, eg wainscot chair.

Introduction to silver

- The value of silver depends on a combination of age, proportion, style, workmanship, balance, weight and patina. Fashions come and go, but quality pieces will always tend to retain value.
- The best silver pieces will have no damage or alteration, will retain original decoration and carry a full set of marks correctly grouped and spaced.
- Patina, due to oxidation, age and handling, should be "glowing" and unblemished. A break in the patination is a sure sign of a repair or an alteration.
- Avoid any pieces that have been "cleaned" with harsh chemicals and have an over-white appearance.
- Poor patina may indicate the use of sub-standard metal; or the piece may be an electroplate copy of a period piece; both of these are typical tell-tale signs of a recent fake.
- Assay and other marks are a helpful guide to dating, but are by no means infallible.
- As a basic rule, the marks should follow the shape of the piece: arranged in a circle on a round-bottomed piece; in a line on a square-bottomed. Each piece of a multipart item should have its own set of marks.

- All legitimate repairs must be separately marked; so new marks on a lid, spout or handle indicate a repair which reduces the value of the piece.
- Look for a patched-on hallmark; junction lines are visible on a tarnished piece when it is breathed on. Or examine under magnification.
- A patched-on hallmark may indicate an attempt to deceive. Between 1719–59 and 1784–90 marks were sometimes taken from a spoon, watch-case or small object, and patched-on to a more substantial piece to avoid duty. Patination can be a helpful guide in distinguishing between the two forms.
- When buying, the absence of assay marks does not necessarily point to a fake on British pieces. Pieces made to commission, or in a place remote from an assay office, may only carry the maker's marks.
- Most countries had their own assay rules, but, there can be exceptions to those rules. If in doubt, always seek expert advice.
- Armorials should be contemporary with the piece. They then add value and are also useful guides to dating and understanding the history of a piece.

Introduction to silver

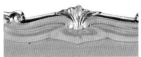

Shell and scroll border, 18thC–present.

Gadroon border, 18thC–present.

Piecrust border, 18thC–present.

- They should also be in original condition; check with a strong magnifying glass for any re-engraving. A second, sharp, engraving line will be seen within the lines of the original decoration if this has happened.
- Armorials were often added later to increase the value of a piece. Such additions are difficult to detect but may be brilliantly sharp compared to other decoration on the piece.
- Armorials, initials, names or dedications were also sometimes erased or replaced as fashions changed, and this can detract from the value.
- Look for signs of a patch or thin sections where the silver has been worn away. Bear in mind that a patch may be difficult to detect if the joins form part of the decoration.
- The areas most susceptible to damage are the joints at handles, spouts and feet, also rims. Check also for pin-prick holes where the silver has thinned through handling or cleaning.
- Always be aware that marriages can be done skilfully and take a variety of forms. One frequently found marriage is a genuinely old hallmarked base or handle married to a later piece; or apostle finials added to other cutlery stems.
- Because of the high price of silver in general, always exercise care when buying, and seek trustworthy advice if in the slightest doubt.

METALWARE

Decoration

ENGRAVING

A sharp tool or 'burin' is used to incise, or scratch, a pattern into the surface. Typical motifs include coats of arms, monograms and floral designs. Technique has been used for centuries and is still used today, although designs are now usually engraved by machine. Patterns typically shallow, not visible on reverse.

BRIGHT CUT

A form of engraving comprised of shallow, faceted cuts into the surface. As they are angled, they reflect the light creating a sparkling effect. Popular from the late 18thC-early 19thC, it is comonly found around the borders of a piece. It may be worn through cleaning and use and such wear reduces value.

ENGINE TURNED

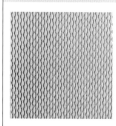

Form of engraving using a machine such as a lathe, where a decorative pattern is incised into the surface. Patterns include plain parallel lines, lines of 'fine barley', fluting and chequer-board and basketweave. Introduced in late 18hC and still used today. Typically found on small items such as snuffboxes and pens.

HAMMERED

Hammers are used to beat dents into heated, pliable silver held against a hard surface. Usually irregularly formed, the dents form a dappled patchwork. Also known as 'martele' or 'planishing', it reached the height of its popularity in the late 19thC Arts & Crafts movement.

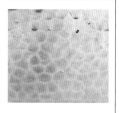

METALWARE

CUT-CARD

A form of strapwork, where shapes of flat silver instead of long straps are cut from a sheet and applied to a flat body with heat. They may be further decorated with engraving or other techniques. Introduced in late 17thC, stylized leaf and geometric forms can be found; complexity grew as period progressed.

REPOUSSÉ

A combination of chasing and embossing. With embossing, a raised design is worked into the reverse of the silver using a hammer or punch. The pattern is visible on the reverse. An embossed design may be refined with chasing, where finer and lower relief details are added by pushing the metal back from the front.

APPLIED

Term used for any decorative or functional component made separately and added to a form. Often cast and further decorated, with handles and finials being examples. Applied borders of repeated beads are known as 'beading', while similar borders of convex lobes or flutes are known as 'gadrooning'.

ENAMELLED

Coloured ground glass is mixed with an oily medium and painted onto surface, then heated to bond. With guilloche enamelling, the underlying metal may be worked with a series of linear cuts to give an added visual effect. Damage expensive to repair, and reduces value considerably.

BATEMAN, HESTER (active 1761-93)

Hester Bateman took over her husband's silversmithing company after his death. She registered her own mark in 1761.

- She ran the company for 30 years, and under her control it became one of the most successful silver workshops in London.

- Hester employed her sons John, Peter and Jonathan.
- Collectors look for tea and coffee pots, spoons and other domestic ware.

BOULTON, MATTHEW (1728-1809)

English metalworker and silversmith, founded a factory in 1762 in Birmingham with John Fothergill producing domestic ware in silver and Sheffield plate. The company continued after his death until the mid-19thC.

- Produced wares in the Adam style.
- Later manufactured mass-produced coins and medals.

CAFÉ, JOHN (active 1740-57), WILLIAM (died c1802)

John Café was an English silversmith best known for his candlesticks.

- After his death, his firm was run by his brother and apprentice William Café.
- The workshop became bankrupt in 1772, although production continued until at least 1784.
- Their work included vinaigrettes, snuff boxes and other small items.

CHASE BRASS & COPPER COMPANY

American manufacturer founded 1876 that made metal household goods from 1930 until the end of WWII.

- Pieces worked in a Modernist, almost Art Deco style.
- Primarily used copper, brass and chromed metal.
- Employed noted designers including Walter von Nessen and Russell Wright.

DIXON, JAMES (1776-1852)

Founded a silversmiths in Sheffield, England, c1806. It became a leading maker of electroplate and Britannia metal wares.

- 1811: Thomas Smith became partner, company name changed to Dixon & Smith. In 1822 Smith left and Dixon's son William joined; company became Dixon & Son, later James Dixon & Son.
- 1849 Electroplating began, used Brittania metal as a base.
  - Dixon ware was never dated, the numerals on individual pieces being the pattern numbers.
  - The company closed c1992.

ELKINGTON & CO.

Leading firm of English silversmiths set up by George Elkington who took out a revolutionary patent on electroplating in 1840.

- In 1842 Josiah Mason joined as partner; company became Elkington, Mason & Co. By 1847 it was producing large quantities of useful and elaborate decorative wares.
- Mason retired in 1856, the company name changing to Elkington & Co.
- George Elkington died in 1865.
- Independent production continued until formation of British Silverware Ltd in 1963 with amalgamation of Elkington, Garrard and Mappin & Webb.

ERP, DIRK VAN (1855-1933)

Dutch metalworker who settled in California in 1885.

- Van Erp initially made small, plainly decorated copperware items as a hobby. By 1908 this had become his main activity with the opening of The Copper Shop in Oakland.
- He is best known for his copper lamps.
- Workshop moved to San Francisco in 1910.
- Van Erp retired in 1929, production was continued at his studio by his son until 1944.

Fabergé, Peter Carl

FABERGÉ, PETER CARL (1846-1920)

Headed one of Europe's most prestigious jewellers of the late
19thC and early 20thC. The company's enamelling and gold-
smithing remain unsurpassed.

- Fabergé trained in St. Petersburg as a goldsmith and jeweller
  before taking over his father's jewellery shop in 1870.
- Under his guidance the company grew into Russia's
  leading firm of jewellers, receiving Imperial
  appointment in 1885 and supplying the
  famous Easter eggs to Alexander III and
  Nicholas II.
- Fame spread through Europe.
- Range of work was wide,
  included boxes, cigarette cases
  and picture frames.

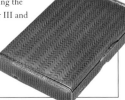

GARRARD II, ROBERT (1793-1881)

Robert Garrard took control of R. & S. Garrard, his father's
London silversmith business in 1818 and developed it into one of
the most prosperous jewellers in Europe. Firm survived until 1952
when it amalgamated with Goldsmith's
and Silversmith's Company.

- Garrard succeeded Philip Rundell as
  royal goldsmith in 1830.
- Firm's success based on utilitarian
  wares yet Garrard's renown rested on
  elaborate commemorative pieces.

GORHAM MANUFACTURING COMPANY

American silversmith company established in Providence, Rhode
Island in c1818 by Jabez Gorham (1792-1869).

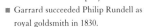

- The firm's expansion and success dates from after 1854 when
  Jabez's son John (1820-98) joined the company and introduced
  mechanical silver production methods for solid
  silver wares.
- Trade and date marks introduced
  from 1868.
- Most pieces based on 18thC designs
  until 1891 when William Codman
  introduced more
  modern designs.
- Gorham is still in
  operation today.

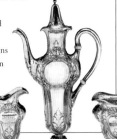

Lamerie, Paul de

JARVIE, ROBERT (1865-1941)

Established the Jarvie Shop in Chicago, US, in 1904, produced Arts & Crafts metalware.

- Specialized in candlesticks but also made a range of useful wares. Elegant, simple shapes often show traces of 18thC style.
  - Most pieces marked "Jarvie" or "Made by the Jarvie Shop". The firm closed in 1917.

JENSEN, GEORG (1866-1935)

Danish jewellery designer and silversmith who produced pieces in a unique form of the Art Nouveau style.

- Jensen established his own workshop in Copenhagen in 1904.
- Initially only produced jewellery but in 1906 produced first holloware and flatware.
- 1907 began partnership with Johan Rohde (1856-1935).
- Later flatware, teapots and coffee-pots distinguished by clean outlines and sense of balance.

- Pieces nearly always marked with Jensen's name or initials.
- Firm is still in operation today.

KALO SHOP

Founded in Chicago, US, by Clara Barck Welles in 1900 to teach and train young women with an interest in Arts & Crafts.

- Produced handmade jewellery and silver and copper tableware.
- Typically favoured geometric shapes and naturalistic decorative motifs.

LAMERIE, PAUL DE (1688-1751)

French-born Huguenot silversmith who moved to England and produced high quality work.

- 1716: became Goldsmith to George I.
- One of the first silver craftsmen to adopt the English Rococo style in the late 1730s.

Liberty & Co

METALWARE

LIBERTY & CO.

London department store, founded in 1875, which promoted artistic innovation.

- Employed leading British Arts & Crafts jewellery designers Archibald Knox (1864-1933), Jessie M. King (1876-1949) and Oliver Baker (1856-1939).
- Cymric gold and silverware and Tudric pewterware ranges introduced early 1900s until c1938.
- The company is still in operation today.

REVERE, PAUL (THE YOUNGER, 1734-1818)

American silversmith and folk hero of the War of Independence.

- Began work as a silversmith in Boston before 1760.
- Career spans the American Colonial and Federal periods and style changes accordingly.
- Best pieces made under the patronage of wealthy American elite.

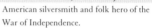

ROYCROFT

Set up by Elbert Green Hubbard (1856-1915) in 1895. The Roycroft Craft Community produced copperware from 1903. Copperware production increased after 1908 with the input of Karl Kip, who had previously worked at the Roycroft bookbinding workshop.

- Items including vases, bowls, bookends, ice buckets, candlesticks, and table lamps sold from the community's shop.

STORR, PAUL (1771-1844)

Englishman who set up a series of successful silver making partnerships and companies from 1792 until his retirement in 1838.

- Produced much work for the royal goldsmiths, Rundell, Bridge & Rundell.

- It is not known how much silver produced by the companies was actually made by Storr.

METALWARE

TIFFANY & CO.

Founded in New York in 1837 as a "fancy goods" store by Charles Louis Tiffany (1812-1902), Tiffany & Co. went on to become America's leading manufacturer of silver, jewellery and glass.

- Initial stock purchased on buying trips to Europe, including pieces from the estate of French Empress Eugénie.
- 1848: shops focusing on jewellery and silver opened in Paris and London.
- 1868: Tiffany purchases silversmith John C. Moore's company, that had previously supplied Tiffany silverware from 1851.
- 1902: Charles' son Louis Comfort Tiffany (1848-1933) took control and became the company's first artistic director. A trained artist, he brought Art Nouveau inspiration to the firm.

- 1950s: saw a move to simpler forms from innovative contemporary artists.
- The company is still in operation today.

UNITE, GEORGE (d.1896)

English silversmith based in Birmingham, which was and continues to be a centre for silverworking, during the 19thC.

- Unite is well known for his small pieces including wine labels, vinaigrettes and vesta cases.
- His work shows great skill in repoussé work and other traditional decorative techniques.

W.M.F.

German firm founded by Daniel Straub, in Geislingen, in 1853.

- 1880: re-named Württembergische Metallwarenfabrik (WMF).
- Known for Art Nouveau metalware.
- Company still active today.

Introduction and understanding hallmarks

Because silver and gold were of commercial importance, it became necessary to create a standard of purity to which everyone must adhere. In England in 1300, a lion's head mark was introduced. Known at the time as a 'leopart', it has evolved into the leopard's head used today. The crown was removed c1821-22. In 1327, a charter empowered the Goldsmith's Company at Goldsmith's Hall in London to test and mark, or 'assay', silver, resulting in the term 'hallmark'. Since then other assay offices have appeared. Look at *Miller's Silver & Silver Plate Marks* to interpret hallmarks.

All British silver, with few exceptions, is hallmarked. There are usually four

symbols, which may be found in any order. Each has its own meaning. From left:

- The maker's mark of the silversmith.
- The 'lion passant', standard purity mark.
- The assay office mark .
- The date letter, indicating the year a piece was marked (and most probably made). The shape and style indicates a particular year. Other marks may also appear in

addition to these four. From 1784-1890, a tax was imposed on silver and to prove the tax had been paid, a fifth mark of the sovereign's head in profile was added. For the first six months of 1785, this was intaglio (fully indented), but after this period, it became cameo (raised), like other marks. The mark above shows George III and was used from mid 1785 until 1820. The

mark left shows Victoria and was used from 1837 until 1890 when the tax was finally abolished.

OTHER MARKS

From 1697-1720, the silver standard was raised and 'Britannia' marks were used (1 & 2). Other marks showing the sovereign's head in profile indicate years of production: George V's silver jubilee 1934-35 (3), Elizabeth II's coronation 1953 (4), and silver jubilee 1977 (5). From 1976, some assay offices in certain countries used a control mark which became legally acceptable internationally (6).

Introduction and understanding hallmarks

MAJOR ASSAY OFFICES (ACTIVE)

*London
1478-1821*

*London
1822-present*

*Birmingham
1773-present*

*Sheffield
1773-present*

*Edinburgh
1485-present*

*Edinburgh
1759-1974*

*Edinburgh
1975-present*

*Dublin
1637-present*

*Dublin
1731-present*

MAJOR ASSAY OFFICES (INACTIVE)

*Chester
1686-1962*

*Exeter
1701-1882*

*Glasgow
1536-1964*

*Newcastle
1423-1884*

*Norwich
17thC*

*Norwich
1423-1697*

*York
1423-1700*

*York
1701-1856*

SILVER IMPORTED INTO BRITAIN

From 1904 all silver imported into the UK had to be marked with its purity, eg; '.925'. In 1973, the decimal point was removed. In addition, a date letter was applied and each UK assay office had its own mark (London shown above left).

European hallmarks

METALWARE

French Hallmarks

Marks were used as early as 1272, but the system was inconsistent. In general, before the French Revolution in 1789, up to four marks were used. These comprise a maker's mark, a community or 'juranada' mark, a city charge mark

and sometimes a related city discharge mark (see below).

FRENCH CITY CHARGE MARKS (PARIS)

Charge Mark 1744-50   *Discharge Mark 1744-50*   *Discharge Mark 1744-50*

SOME FRENCH POST-REVOLUTIONARY MARKS

Head 1793-97   *Cockerel 1798-1819*   *Head 1809-19*   *Old Man 1819-38*

Old Man 1819-38   *Old Man 1819-38*   *Minerva 1879 onwards*   *Minerva 1879 onwards*

SOME GERMAN CITY MARKS

Berlin 18thC   *Berlin 19thC*   *Dresden 19thC*   *Frankfurt 17th/18thC*

Hamburg 18thC   *Munich 18thC*   *Nuremberg 19thC*   *Stuttgart 19thC*

European hallmarks

OTHER EUROPEAN SILVER MARKS

In general, marking systems used by European countries were inconsistent, if they existed at all. Many marks are of little use, but city or country marks may be more reliable. Some of the many examples are shown below.

Florence
17th-18thC

Milan
c1810

Rome
Late 17thC

Turin
18th - 19thC

Italy
After 1934

Italy
After 1934

Amsterdam
assay mark

The Hague,
assay mark

Rotterdam
assay mark

Netherlands
after 1953

Netherlands
after 1953

Lisbon,
Early 19thC

Moscow
c1880

St Petersburg
dated 1742

Russia
1882 onwards

Russia
1896-1908

Moscow
dated 1782

Russia
1908-17

USSR
1927-58

Barcelona
18thC

Madrid
late 18thC

Spain
after 1881

Spain
after 1881

Stockholm,
18th-19thC

Zurich
18thC

Geneva
19thC

Switzerland
1882-1934

Switzerland
1882-1934

Gold & platinum marks

BRITISH GOLD MARKS

Like silver marks, gold marks were introduced in 1300, with the earliest being a leopard's head (*see p170*). A maker's mark was also required from 1363, and a date letter from 1578. From 1544, the leopard's head was replaced with a lion passant.

In 1477, the standard was reduced from 19⅕ to 18 carats, which lasted until 1575 when it was superceded by the current 22 carat standard. In 1798, the lower 18 carat standard was re-introduced, and indicated by a crown mark. This remained until 1844. The crown was then used for both standards.

In 1854, three more standards were introduced: 9, 12 and 15 carat. The standard was indicated by both a figure and a percentage. These were used until 1932 when the 12 and 15 carat standards were replaced by 14 carat.

22 carat to 1974	22 carat 1975-present	Foreign imports
18 carat to 1974	18 carat 1975-present	Foreign imports
14 carat to 1974	14 carat 1975-present	Foreign imports
9 carat to 1974	9 carat 1975-present	Foreign imports

Edinburgh (replaces crown)	*Glasgow* (replaces crown)	*Glasgow* (replaces crown)

Gold & platinum marks

METALWARE

GOLD AND PLATINUM ASSAY OFFICE MARKS

Birmingham

Chester

Dublin

Edinburgh

Exeter

Glasgow

London

Newcastle

Sheffield

York

IMPORTED FOREIGN PIECES

From 1842 pieces were hallmarked. From 1876, an 'F' was included. From 1904, each assay office used its own mark.

Birmingham

Chester

Edinburgh

Glasgow

London

Sheffield

PLATINUM MARKS

Platinum came under hall-marking law in 1973. Since 1975, all UK platinum wares have been marked with orb, date and assay office marks.

Birmingham

Date letter

Imported

London

Orb

Sheffield

INTERNATIONAL GOLD MARKS

As with silver marks, few countries have adopted a reliable, consistent policy of marking their gold wares. In general, '750' should indicate 18ct gold, '585' 14ct gold, and '375' 9ct gold. US marks may read '14KT' for 14ct gold. However, '14KR' indicates 14 carat rolled (plated) gold. Always consult a specialist book to ensure accuracy.

US marks

The word 'STERLING' in capital letters generally indicates that a silver object was made in the US.

However, not all pieces bear this word, and other marks are known.

Many pieces are simply marked with a maker's mark. Unlike the UK, the name often appears in full within a border, rather than as initials.

A symbol may also be used, such as the knight on horseback mark (left),

which was the symbol for Mary C. Knight, or the capital 'S' in a shield symbol (below), which was used by Simons Bros. Some 19thC

and 20thC items may also bear a retailer's name. Date letters were not used, and although some pieces may bear a State mark, town and city marks

were often inconsistent. Major makers include Jeremiah Dummer (1645-1718), who is

credited with being the first US-born silversmith, Robert Sanderson (1608-93), the Gorham Manufacturing Co. (see p166) and Paul Revere (see p168). During the early 20thC, many silversmiths

turned to the Arts & Crafts style of the period. Major makers included Tiffany (see below), Robert Jarvie (see p167) and The Kalo Shop (see p167). Many of these makers used the word 'Sterling' in their marks, and its useage continues today.

TIFFANY SILVER MARKS

Until 1851, when Tiffany partnered with silver-smiths J.C. Moore, the company used a number of US companies to produce its silver. The "G&W" mark (above right) indicates Grosjean & Woodward. Pattern and order numbers also marked, and can help identify when a piece was made. Used .925 standard from 1851.

Canadian & Mexican silver

CANADIAN SILVER

As many 18thC silversmiths were French Huguenots, Canada used marks similar to France; the first letters of the maker's name in a shield surmounted by a crown, fleur de lys or star. After British rule began in 1763, the marks lost their heraldic motifs and the shield became a rectangle or semi-circle. In the early 19thC many marks imitated British hallmarks. The words 'Montreal' or 'Quebec' may be added as as well as 'Sterling'.

Major 19thC makers include Robert Hendery and John Leslie, whose company was acquired by Birks (mark below) in 1898. From 1908 the .925 standard was a legal requirement. Carl Petersen (1895-1977) worked in the Georg Jensen style (mark above top).

MEXICAN SILVER

Although Mexican silver is marked, the system is inconsistant. 'Mexico Silver' or 'Silver Made In Mexico' marks are often accompanied by a number indicating purity. This varies, but is usually at or above the .925 standard. Eagle marks were used from 1948 until the 1970s. The integral number indicates the city of assay, with '1' for Mexico City, and '3' for Taxco. A maker's mark may also be found. One of the most sought after is Spratling.

OTHER US METALWARE

During the 19thC and 20thC, many US companies worked with other metals, including copper, bronze, sterling silver on bronze, and silver plate. Notable names include Tiffany (see p169), The Roycrofters (see p168 and mark above), Dirk van Erp, (see p165) and Heintz Art Metal Co. (right). Many followed the Arts & Crafts or Art Nouveau styles.

Silver teapot dates and shapes

METALWARE

Queen Anne octagonal baluster, UK

George I bullet, UK

George III oval Rococo, UK

George III bombé Rococo, UK

George III shaped oval, UK

George III shaped oval, UK

George III classical vase-shaped, UK

George III oval oblong, UK

George IV oblong, UK

George IV compressed round, UK

Victorian circular tapered, UK

Mid 19thC Victorian oval straight-sided, UK

Victorian baluster, UK

Late 19thC 'Aesthetic' canted rectangular, UK

Victorian Rococo Revival, UK

Silver coffeepot dates and shapes

*Early 18thC
panelled-form, UK*

*George II tapering,
UK*

*George II Rococo,
UK*

*George II baluster,
UK*

*George III Rococo,
UK*

*George III baluster,
UK*

*George III baluster
Rococo, UK*

*George III tapering,
UK*

*George III baluster,
UK*

*George III baluster
Rococo, UK*

*Early 19thC Empire
classical oval, US*

*Mid 19thC classical
baluster, France*

*Mid 19thC classical
urn form, US*

*Late 19thC Victorian
tapering, UK*

*Late 19thC classical
straight tapering, US*

Silver candlestick dates and shapes

METALWARE

Mid 15thC,
England

Mid 16thC,
England

Mid 18thC,
France

Mid 18th, UK

Mid 18thC,
Germany

Mid 18thC,
UK

Late 18thC,
UK

Late 18thC,
France

Late 18thC,
France

Late 18thC,
UK

Late 18thC,
UK

Early 19thC,
UK

Mid 19thC,
Austria

Mid 19thC,
UK

Late 19thC,
Germany

Late 19thC,
UK

Late 19thC,
Poland

Late 19thC,
UK

Early 20thC,
Germany

Early 20thC,
Germany

Silver mugs & sauce boats dates and shapes

Early 18thC George I tapering, UK

Mid 18thC baluster-shape, UK

Late 18thC baluster-shape, UK

Late 18thC George III baluster, UK

Early 19thC straight sided, UK

Mid 19thC Rococo Revival, UK

Mid 19thC baluster renaissance revival, UK

Late 19thC Victorian baluster, UK

Late 19thC 'Morning Glory', UK

Mid 18thC George II plain bulbous form, hoof feet, UK

Mid 18thC George II Rococo form, pad feet, UK

Mid 18thC George II fluted bellied oval form, UK

Mid 18thC George III oval form, on shell and hoof feet, UK

Late 18thC George III oval helmet form, trifid feet, UK

Late 18thC George III oval form, shell and hoof feet, UK

Early 19thC George III oval pedestal form, UK

Late 19thC Victorian oval form, UK

Early 20thC silver plain bulbous form, US

Silver plate

METALWARE

Old Sheffield Plate

- The process of fusing a thin sheet of silver to a thicker of copper dates from mid-18thC. By 1800, a wide range of articles were being produced.
- Platers copied popular styles, and the styles of 'Queen Anne' and 'Early Georgian' were made into the early 19thC. Such articles cannot, because of the process, be earlier than the 1740s.
- In the early 19thC, Empire style pieces were embellished with heavy ornamental designs made possible by the increasing use of plated wire.

An early period old Sheffield plated two handled cup. c1765

- British Plate: a process patented in 1836. The copper element in silver plating was replaced with 'German silver', a silver-coloured alloy which contained no actual silver. Because it was cheaper, tougher and did not have the reddish copper to show through when worn, it brought about the end of

Sheffield plate production by the 1840s when it was superseded by the even cheaper electro-plating method.

- Electro-plated articles from mid-19thC onwards are often referred to as 'Sheffield Plate'. By law the term should only be applied to wares in which

Two middle period old Sheffield plated tankards. c1790

silver has been fused to copper. Only such wares should be so marked.

- On hollow ware a useful test is to check for a seam. Electro-plating covers a piece completely. If there is no seam the piece is unlikely to be old Sheffield plate.
- The words 'Sheffield Plated' indicate that the piece is electro-plated and not genuine old Sheffield plate. Such a piece dates from mid-19thC.
- In North America articles made by fusing or depositing a layer of silver onto base metal are called 'silver plate'.

Silver plate

Dating Sheffield Plate

- Sheared edges c1745-1760: metal plated on one side, revealing copper edge.

A pair of late period old Sheffield plated candlesticks. c1830

- Single lapped edges c1760-1890: silver layer was extended to lap over and conceal copper edge.
- Double lapped edges, c1770-1810: silvered copper ribbons soldered to edges to lap over on to copper undersides.
- Silver lapped edges, c1775-1815: both sides of copper sheet silver-plated. U-shaped silver wire used to conceal any copper revealed by shearing. Joins almost invisible.
- After 1815: ornamentation more elaborate.

Marks

- No marks legally permitted before 1784.
- After that date makers could use individual symbols. However, some continued to sell their goods unmarked.
- Registration of marks ceased in 1835.
- From 1820 to 1835 fine quality Sheffield plate could carry a crown mark to distinguish it from lightly-silvered imports, particularly from France.
- After 1820 makers stamped some of their products with a mark indicating the proportion of silver and copper.
- Simulated silver hallmarks, normally consisting of five marks, appear on Sheffield plate from c1836.

A rare Hukin & Heath electro-plated spoonwarmer.

- After 1836: marks on British plate imitated silver hallmarks.

A late 19thC pair of silver plated wine coolers.

Pewter

- Pewter is an alloy of tin and other metals, notably lead or antimony and/or copper and/or bismuth. Fine old pewter is an alloy of tin and copper, but the three most common types of period pewter are: lay or ley, trifle, and hard metal or plate pewter.

- Because of the range and quantity of items made over 500 years, it is impossible to give precise rules for identifying and dating by means of marks. Many domestic items were not marked at all, particularly when produced outside London, Philadelphia and other main centres.

- Where marks do appear, they are not always what they seem and other factors (shape, patina etc.) should always be considered when trying to date. Forged marks, added in 20thC, are not unknown.

- hence the term "Touchmark" for such makers' stamps (which were impressed, never engraved).

- The touchmark plates dating from the late 15thC were destroyed in the Great Fire of London in 1666. The plates now in existence date from 1668 when the system was revived.

- The earliest touchmarks were small and normally consisted of the pewterer's initials. Generally, the smaller the mark, the earlier the item. They were usually struck on handles, or the front rims of flatware.

- Subsequently, touchmarks became more elaborate, often incorporating pictorial designs or symbols. Full names appear, sometimes with addresses. These larger

TOUCHMARKS

- The most consistently helpful of marks on English pewter are the makers' marks which the Pewterers' Company in London compelled its members to use.

- Each pewterer had his individual mark which was registered on special plates known as "Touch Plates" –

- marks are stamped on the underside of plates, and on the lids, or inside the bases of tankards.

- When a date is included, this indicates when the touch was registered and not when the piece was made.

- Touchmarks ceased to be registered in 1824.

Pewter

QUALITY MARKS

Quality marks

- Touchmarks do not indicate the quality of the alloy, although they do suggest craftsmanship.
- Neither lay (the lowest quality) or trifle pewter carried quality marks, but hard metal pieces were marked with an X.
- From mid 18thC, the best quality plate pewter was marked with an X surmounted by a crown.
- From late 17thC quality export pieces should be marked with a "Rose and Crown" stamp. In 18thC this mark was used on pieces for sale in Britain.

IMITATION MARKS

Imitation hallmarks

- These appear on many 18thC pieces. They copied genuine silver marks in design and positioning. Though crude they can provide useful clues to period and maker.

Other marks

- Coats of arms, owner's initials, etc, can all be of use in confirming the period of a piece. However, be sure the mark was not added later.

Britannia metal

- Superior form of pewter evolved in the late 18thC from plate pewter. It was widely used in 19thC.
- Pieces were marked with names or trademarks on the underside.
- If the mark includes a pattern number, it is Britannia metal.

EXCISE MARKS

Excise marks

- After 1824, all measures and drinking vessels in which liquor was sold by measure, had to be tested and stamped with a mark. These marks varied from area to area. However, after 1877 the mark was standardized to a crown, monarch's initial, town number and sometimes a date letter.

AMERICAN PEWTER

American pewter

- Until c1750 most pewter came from Europe. Early US pewterers used or adapted touches they had brought with them, or designed their own.

Glossary

METALWARE

andiron Iron support for wooden logs burning in a fire, used until 18thC instead of a grate; in 17thC they were often just decorative.

apostle spoon Common till early 17thC, spoon with figure of an apostle as finial.
argyle Spouted pots, made from c1750 to c1830, with two layers or skins, to keep contents hot.

biggin Small teapot or coffee-pot, sometimes with a stand and spirit-lamp, named after inventor George Biggin.
brandy saucepan Small bulbous or baluster-shaped saucepan, usually with handle at right angles to the pouring spout.
bright-cut Silver effect popular in the last years of 18thC, achieved by an engraving technique which made the design stand out more brilliantly than usual.
Britannia metal Cheaper substitute for silver, actually a form of pewter, employed in the first half of 19thC.

British plate Substitute for silver employed in second quarter of 19thC, until superseded by electro-plating. Often carries marks resembling silver hallmarks.
caddy Container for tea.
caddy spoon Spoon for taking tea out of the caddy, with a short handle and a large bowl, often decorated. Introduced late 18thC.

canteen Either a large urn with a tap at the bottom; or a case containing a silver service.
card case Case for visiting cards, popular in silver from c1820 into the 20thC.
cartouche Frame or surround as decoration round eg a coat-of-arms engraved on a piece.
caster or castor Vessel for sprinkling, usually pepper or sugar.
caudle cup Covered cup for a warm drink, whether caudle (spiced gruel laced with wine or ale) or some other.
centrepiece Ornament designed to occupy centre of dining table.
chafing dish Stand for dishes and plates, incorporating a spirit lamp to keep them warm. From mid 17thC.
chased Decorated and

worked, usually with hammer and punches, but not carved, cut away or engraved. Flat chasing is chasing in very low relief.

chenet French andiron, of a type common in 17thC, often elaborately decorated.

claret jug Ewer or jug used

for serving claret in 19thC, but not easy to distinguish from ewers made for other purposes.

coaster Saucer or small tray for a bottle, on which it was passed or slid round the table (some have wheels).

counter box Box, usually

round, for storing counters or tokens used in gambling. From 17thC.

cow creamer Jug for pouring cream modelled in the shape of a cow, popular in 18thC.

cruet Frame holding salt cellars and other vessels containing condiments, or for casters.

cut-card work Silver decoration achieved by applying or overlaying the silver body with a second, patterned piece or sheet (often fretted) of silver. Common in 17thC, particularly with Huguenot craftsmen.

damascene Inlay of precious metal (gold, silver) on to another metal (steel), a craft in which Syrian Muslims excelled (in and around Damascus: hence the name).

dinanderie Vessel or other object of brass, made in the factories in Dinant near Liege, France, in 15thC.

douter Implement resembling scissors, for snuffing out a candle flame.

dram cup Small cup with two handles, common in second half of 17thC. Also called porringers.

electroplate To cover one metal with a thin layer of another – usually silver plated over an alloy body. Process was patented in the 1830s, and gradually superseded Sheffield plate.

embossed Having a relief ornament, achieved by hammering the metal into shape from its reverse side.

épergne Type of centrepiece featuring a large central bowl and several smaller ones.

Glossary

étui Small box for holding useful items, from pins to scissors to pencils. 18thC.

everted Outward-turned or flaring, eg a rim.

finial Endpiece, eg at the top of a spoon handle.

freedom box Silver box bestowed with the "freedom" of a city, in late 18thC and early 19thC.

jardinière Ornamental pot or vase for flowers or plants.

latten The old English word for what is now called brass.

mazarine Strainer, typically oval, fitting over a dish into which meat or fish drained. From mid 18thC.

mount Metal fitment or adjunct.

nutmeg grater Box containing nutmeg and a grater, usually for sprinkling nutmeg on ale. 18thC.

obverse Of a coin or medal; the front side, opposite to the reverse.

patch-box Box, often round, for ladies' "beauty spots" or patches. 17thC.

pepperette Vessel for sprinkling pepper.

pewter Alloy of tin and lead (and usually a variety of other metals), used for table utensils and other vessels until into 19thC.

porringer Cup, usually quite large, with two handles and a cover, originally for holding porridge or gruel.

pounce box Cylinder or bottle with sprinkler for "pounce", a powder used before blotting paper was invented. 18thC.

punch bowl Large bowl on a stepped or moulded foot, usually with two ring handles. End of 17thC.

relief Proudness from the surface; or the apparent volume of a figure modelled on a surface.

repoussé Meaning "pushed out", this is another term for embossed. More exactly, it is the secondary process of chasing the metal that has been embossed, to refine the design further.

salt A bowl for salt may be called simply "a salt".

salver Flat dish or tray on which to place other dishes.

scalloped With a series of circular edges like those of a scallop shell.

sconce Plate for attachment to wall, bearing one or more candle-holders. From 17thC.

scroll Anything that winds or unwinds, creating a loop.

Sheffield plate Rolled sheet silver sandwiching an internal layer of copper, to which it is fused. The process was invented in Sheffield and recognised by the Sheffield assay office in 1784, though Sheffield plate was being made at Sheffield and elsewhere (eg Birmingham) by the 1760s.

sparrow-beak jug Jug with a simple, triangular spout.
standish An inkstand.

stirrup cup Cup used for drinking prior to making a journey or going hunting. Usually shaped as the head of an animal, eg a fox. From second half 18thC.
swagged With applied strips formed in a mould, but not necessarily in a swag or hanging garland shape.
tankard Large mug with a hinged lid and thumbpiece, for drinking beer.
thumbpiece Flange attached to a hinged lid, which, when pressed by the thumb, raises the lid.
tine Prong of a fork.

tôle peinte Sheet iron subjected to a varnish developed in France in mid 18thC, allowing it to be painted on.

touch mark Maker's individual mark stamped on much, but not all, early English pewter.
trefid 17thC spoon of which the handle terminates in the shape of a bud, typically cleft or grooved into a central stem and two lobes.
trembleuse Stand with feet on which to place a cup.
tureen Large bowl (eg for soup), usually on a foot, often with handles. Popular early 18thC.
uniface Medal modelled only on one side.
vesta case Silver matchbox for early vesta matches, which were easily flammable and needed such protection. Popular second half 19thC, in many shapes and designs.

vinaigrette Small box to hold a sponge soaked in vinegar; 18thC equivalent of smelling salts.

Introduction

CLOCKS

- Best prices are paid for working clocks in original condition. Restoring a non-working clock is expensive and even a skilful restoration will never regain the full original value.
- Faces should show the signs appropriate to age. Painted dials should show crazing, or hairline cracks. Wooden faces should have cracks where the timbers have shrunk. Metal faces should have proper oxidation; if the dial has been cleaned, check the reverse side.

A George III oak eight-day longcase clock. c1770

- Plain metal dials were sometimes engraved at a later date to enhance the value. Be wary of a face that seems too elaborate for the case and chapter ring. Generally, the more ornate the half hour marks, the more elaborate the face will be overall.

- Check the back of the dial for blocked holes. These usually indicate the marriage of an unrelated

A George II brass and silvered brass clock face. c1725

dial and movement.
- They may also indicate the marriage of a chapter ring and dial plate. Check the correcting feet are in their original holes and decoration is compatible.
- Sometimes holes are filled legitimately; where mistakes were made by the maker, or a worn post has been removed. Nevertheless, as a rule, beware blocked holes that cannot be explained.
- Replaced hands do not usually diminish value, provided they are compatible in style and quality with the face.
- Examine the movement for consistent colour to all parts and signs of wear appropriate to age.
- Check that the bell is original and not cracked.

Introduction

- Avoid 19thC dial clocks with painted dials in favour of earlier wood, brass or silvered dials; but check for filled holes indicative of an early dial added to later movement.

A tortoiseshell and pique table clock, with silver frame. 1913

A George III mahogany bracket clock. c1820

- Carriage clocks have been mass produced since the mid 19thC. The face should be of enamel and smooth, not thin and corrugated. Modern faces are brilliant white with dense black numerals.
- Side glasses were sometimes replaced by solid gilt panels, which will be different in colour to the case, or painted porcelain. Both detract from value.
- It is impossible to convert from petite to grande sonnerie mode, though attempts have been made. Only an original grande sonnerie carriage is capable of striking in this mode for seven days without rewinding.

A 19thC French porcelain and gilt bronze clock garniture.

Novelty clocks

- The majority of curiosity and mystery clocks date from the 19thC.
- With mystery clocks the movement is disguised so the eye cannot preceive how the hands move.
- Demand for skeleton clocks has increased the number made anew from

A French glass-dialled mystery clock with glass column. c1845

disparate parts. Originals have delicate, finely pierced wheels with at least four spokes.
- The size and shape of the glass dome should be in proportion to the clock; the base should be marble or contemporary wood.
- Alteration to the clock feet, to raise or lower the height, is a sign that clock and dome were not made for each other.

A mid 19thC British brass skeleton clock.

HINTS FOR DATING BRACKET CLOCKS

Dials

Square	to c1770
Broken arch	from c1720
Round/painted/silvered	from c1760

Case finish

Ebony veneer	from c1660 to c1850
Walnut	from c1670 to c1870
Marquetry	from c1680 to c1740
Rosewood	from c1790
Lacquered	from c1700 to c1760
Mahogany	from c1730

Bracket clock styles

*Late 17thC
Lantern clock*

*Late 17thC
British*

*Late 17thC
Louis XIV, France*

*Late 18thC
Louis XVI, France*

*Late 18thC
George III, UK*

*Early 19thC
William IV, UK*

*Early 19thC
Regency, UK*

*Early 19thC
Federal, US*

*Mid 19thC
ormolu, France*

*Late 19thC
Victorian, UK*

*Late 19thC carriage
clock, France*

*Late 19thC
Gothic Revival*

*Late 19thC
Aesthetic Movement*

*Late 19thC Neo-
classical style, France*

*Early 20thC
Arts & Crafts, UK*

Longcase clock styles

Early 18thC Queen Anne, UK

Mid 18thC George II, UK

Late 18thC Chippendale, US

Late 18thC George III, UK

Late 18thC George III Japanned, UK

18thC Marquetry, Holland

Early 19thC Federal, US

Early 19thC Regency, UK

Early 19thC William IV, UK

Mid19thC Victorian, UK

Late 19thC Louis XVI Style, France

Early 20thC Arts & Crafts UK

Dating longcase clocks

c1700
square brass

early 18thC
square brass

c1740 brass
break-arch

late 18thC
moonphase

c1790
silvered dial

c1820
circular, painted

HINTS FOR DATING LONG/TALLCASE CLOCKS

Case finish

	Ebony veneer	up to c1725
	Walnut veneer	from c1670 to c1770
	Lacquered	from c1700 to c1790
	Mahogany	from 1730
	Softwood	from c1690
	Mahogany inlay	from c1750
	Marquetry	from c1680 to c1760
	Oak	always
Dials	8in (20.5cm) square	to c1669
	10in (25.5cm) square	from c1665-1800
	11in (28cm) square	from 1690-1800
	12in (30.5cm) square	from c1700
	14in (35.5cm) square	from c1740
	Broken-arch dial	from c1715
	Round dial	from c1760
	Silvered dial	from c1760
	Painted dial	from c1770
	Hour hand only	to 1820
	Minute hand introduced	c1663
	Second hand	from 1675
	Matching hands	from c1775

Wall clock styles & dating

*Late18thC
Act of Parliament*

*Late 18thC
Louis XVI cartel*

*Early 19thC Federal,
US*

*Early 19thC banjo,
US*

*Early 19thC
Regency, UK*

*Early 19thC
William IV, UK*

*Mid-19thC to 20thC
Vienna-style*

*Late 19thC
Black Forest*

*Mid 19thC to early
20thC Dial, UK*

HINTS FOR DATING WALL CLOCKS		
Case finish	Ebony veneer	from c1690
	Marquetry	from c1680 to c1695
	Mahogany	from c1740
	Oak	always
Dials	Square	to c1755
	Broken arch	from c1720 to c1805
	Painted/round	from c1740
	Silvered	from c1760

Identifying makers

A Philadephia tall case clock by Edward Duffield. c1740

- In Britain from 1698 every clock dial had to be marked with the maker's name and place of origin. In the 19thC however, the name that appears is sometimes that of an English importer and not of the continental maker.
- A clock made after 1698 may also carry the retailer's name; if the face is silver it too may carry maker's marks.
- These marks are important clues to the origin and value of the piece, and there is much information on makers which will help in assessing rarity and value.
- The position of the signature varies with the type of clock, but usually appears on the dial and/or the backplate.
- However, be aware that makers' names may be added to an unsigned clock, or engraved over a previously erased

signature, usually to enhance value by the addition of a more collectable name.
- Such additions can be difficult to detect; familiarity with a maker's work is necessary to judge whether the quality and style is right for the name it bears.
- On a metal face, look for hammer marks on the back, or signs of thinning where metal was beaten to erase an original name.
- Another way to detect a "new" name is to feel the engraving: old engraving feels smooth, whereas new work feels sharp.
- Clocks signed "Thomas Moore, Ipswich" are particularly numerous modern pieces, treated to look old.
- On carriage clocks, a serial number on the back plate of more than five digits is modern.
- Clock cases were made separately from the mechanism and are almost never signed.

"Vulliamy" signature and date on a bulk head timepiece.

Pocket watches

- Pocket watches were first made during the second half of the 16thC, and used a verge escapement. Watches of this date have only one hand, a typical feature until late 17thC.

An early 18thC French verge pocket watch.

The watch above, opened and showing the movement.

- During the second half of the 18thC, watches became more available.
- At the start of the 19thC, watches became slimmer; the more efficient lever escapement took over from the cylinder escapement in the 1830s.
- 'Keyless' watches with an inbuilt winding mechanism were introduced during the mid 19thC.

A late 19thC open-faced Swiss pocket watch with gold case.

- The late 19thC saw the greatest number being made. Three main case types: open faced, 'hunter' with flip-up hinged full cover and 'half hunter', with a circular window in the cover.
- Watches with complex mechanisms or added features (such as moon-phases), those by major makers (such as Breguet), and those cased in precious materials or with fine deco-ration will be more desir-able and valuable. Many examples are gold plated or silver plated, and generally of limited value.

An Elgin 'hunter' pocket watch, with gold-filled case. c1910

Wristwatches

Watches were first worn on the wrist in the early 20thC. Many look like pocket watches with wire fittings holding the strap. They became widespread following WWI, and by the 1930s, greatly outnumbered pocket watches.

Watches from the 1930s tend to be cased in Art Deco style square or rectangular cases. Automatic watches were developed c1926. Military examples usually have black dials and robust steel cases. By the 1950s, elegance had returned, as had innovation in terms of display and case design.

Examples with complex mechanisms are more desirable, as are those by major makers (like Patek Phillipe), or those with cases made from precious materials.

*1910s-c1920
pocket watch style*

*1920s
cushion case*

*1930s
Art Deco*

*1940s
military*

*1950s-1960s
classic style*

*1950s
novelty case*

*1950s-70s
mystery dial*

*1950s-70s direct
reader or 'jump'*

*Late 1960s-70s
oversized*

BAROMETERS

Introduction

A George III mahogany cistern tube stick barometer. c1780

- Early instruments should show correct patination to the wood, greeny-brown oxidation to metal (not the black of modern chemical patination) and mellow gold gilding.
- Wheel (banjo) barometers came into popular use in late 18thC, and were mass produced from mid 19thC.
- Early aneroid barometers

Silvered vernier register on stick barometer. c1765

- From the late 17thC barometers were important pieces of domestic equipment, and more common than is generally realized.
- Early types were stick, pediment or diagonal.
- At first the wood mounts were of walnut, but later maple, mahogany, ebony and rosewood were used.

are comparatively rare.
- Barometers normally bear the maker's name and mark, sometimes accompanied by a date and/or registration number.
- Marine and other special types are worth more than domestic versions.

A rosewood mercury wheel barometer. c1843

Types of barometers

Late 17thC cistern tube stick

Late 18thC Georgian angle

Late 18thC Georgian cistern stick

Late 18th-19thC stick barometer

Mid-19thC Victorian marine stick

Early 19thC wheel

19thC Victorian 'five dial' wheel

Late 19th-early 20thC pocket aneroid

Late19th-early 20thC wall aneroid

Late 19thC Victorian wheel

c1900 Admiral Fitzroy

Late 19thC barograph

Introduction

A 19thC French armillary sphere, on a fruitwood base.

- The finest and earliest instruments are so rare that anything offered as pre-18thC should be treated with caution.
- Notable instruments have been copied for a variety of reasons, some legitimate, and these copies may be valuable.

A brass sundial, with a hinged circular dial. c1760

- Value depends on maker, age, materials, decoration, quality and condition. Restoration should ideally be visible; while complete

An early 19thC Bate 'Jones Most Improved' brass microscope.

and working pieces fetch more, there is a market for skilled restorations. Patina should never be removed.

- Armillary spheres show the movement of the planets. Pre-Copernican examples, with the earth in the centre, are virtually all recent copies. 18thC examples are most in demand, while clockwork versions (orreries) are worth many times more than hand-turned.
- Michael Butterfield, the first maker of Butterfield pocket sundials, died in 1724, but there are 18thC and 19thC versions. Originals are rare.
- The most valuable compasses are those made between the mid-17thC and early 19thC. Less decorative 19thC compasses, liquid compasses, and later card examples are inexpensive.
- Pre-1745 microscopes are rare and require expert appraisal before buying. After that date they began to be made in quantity,

Introduction

brass mounted on a box base with an accessory drawer. The Culpeper-type with S-shaped legs can also be valuable. Cased 19thC compound and binocular microscopes with accessories fetch the most.

A pocket sextant, by Geo. Stebbing, Portsmouth.

■ The octant (one-eigth of a circle), invented by Hadley in 1731, was followed by the sextant (one-sixth of a

An 18thC ebony octant, with brass mounts and bone scale.

circle) invented by Campbell in 1757. Both measure angular distance and were made until early 20thC. Early wooden examples are rare. Brass was commoner after 1780; the most valuable examples feature maritime engraving. Ivory, ebony, silver and platinum parts add value.

■ Precision theodolites for measuring weight and orientation were made from 1730. Pre-1840 versions by leading makers command a premium over

utilitarian, but more accurate, later models.

■ After 1750, John Dollond's achromatic lenses cured many of the problems connected with early telescopes and led to many more being made; handmade 18thC mahogany and brass examples have greatest appeal.

■ Decoration and famous names add value. Machine made 19thC and 20thC telescopes are inexpensive, unless they have insignia or an owner's name. Avoid any telescope with damaged lenses or dented cases.

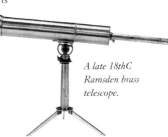

A late 18thC Ramsden brass telescope.

Glossary

anchor escapement
Escapement invented in
England c1670. Named after
the anchor shape of the
linkage between the pallets
controlling the escape wheel.
arbor Clockmaker's term
for the axle on which a wheel
is mounted.
arch Specifically, the arch
above the dial, usual in
longcase clocks from c1700.
backplate The rear of the
two plates supporting the
movement, on which
details of the maker are
often engraved.

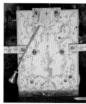

balance Device counteracting
the force of the mainspring on
the crown or balance wheel.
balance spring Spring acting
on the balance wheel to coun-
teract the force of the mainspring, the equivalent in
watches of the pendulum, and
developed shortly after c1675.
barrel Specifically, the barrel
containing the mainspring
round which the string
driving the train is wound.
bezel The metal rim to a glass
cover, eg over a clock face.
Bim Bam Onomatopoeic
name for strike of a type of
German mantel clock popular
in England in early 20thC. It
sounds two strokes of
different tone for the hour.

bimetallic balance
Compensated balance – the
equivalent of a compensated
pendulum – made of brass
and steel. Have different rates
of expansion, so cancel out.

Black Forest Clocks Clocks
were produced in Bohemia
from mid-17thC, but the
usual Black Forest clock with
automata of various kinds
(the most famous of which is
the cuckoo, which appeared
c1730) date from 18thC and
19thC.
bob The weight at the end of
the pendulum.
broken arch Specifically, the
arch to the top of a longcase
clock that is less than a semi-
circle – a sign that it is likely
to be early Georgian (mid-
18thC) in date.
Bun foot Type of foot used on

early longcase clocks.
Caddy top Used on many
early longcase clocks; shaped
like a tea container.
calendar aperture Opening in

the dial displaying the day and month.

chain fusee A fusee from

which a chain (rather than a gutstring) unwinds onto the barrel of the mainspring.

chapter ring The part of the dial on which the numbers of the hours are inscribed.

chronometer Precision timepiece for navigation or science.

compensated pendulum Pendulum which compensates for the changes in its length caused by changes in temperature.

countwheel strike Mechanism that determines the number of strikes for each hour.

date aperture See calendar aperture.

deadbeat escapement Improved version of anchor escapement invented c1715.

dialplate Front plate of the clock, on which chapter ring may be attached or painted.

Dutch strike Chiming system that strikes the next hour at the half-hour. Common on Dutch and German clocks.

eight-day movement Movement requiring winding every eight days.

equation dial Dial with which to equate the time registered

on a sundial and mechanical "mean" time. One hand points to the day, another hand indicates how fast or slow the sundial is.

fusee A grooved spool, from which a line or chain unwinds as it is pulled by the mainspring of the movement.

gridiron pendulum Pendulum made up of several rods, of steel or iron descending from above, and brass rising from the bottom ends of the iron rods. Brass expands in heat more than iron, and so the length of the pendulum is kept constant.

hunter Watch with an opening front cover which protects the glass over the dial.

lantern clock So called from their resemblance to ships' lanterns, these clocks were made in England from c1600 into the 18thC. Driven by weights, not a spring, and marking only the hours, they were replaced by longcase and bracket clocks.

lever escapement A modification of the anchor escapement for watches (or carriage clocks). Escape wheel is restrained by oscillating lever.

Glossary

marine chronometer Precision clock for use at sea.

moonwork Mechanism to count and display the phases and age of the moon.

musical clock Clock with a train driving a cylinder with pins that strike bells to play a selection of tunes.

orrery Named after the fourth Earl of Orrery, an astronomical clock that shows the positions of the sun, moon, earth and sometimes also planets.

overcoil A second spring acting on the balance spring to ensure its concentric winding and unwinding, invented late 18thC.

pair-case Casing that was common on continental watches and standard for English watches from mid 17thC into 19thC: a double case, an inner one for the movement and an outer one that was usually decorated.

pallet Arm or lever that engages in an escapement wheel to halt it.

pillar One of the rods or rivets connecting the dial-plate and the backplate of a movement. The number and shape of these pillars (four, five; ringed, baluster, etc.) are a guide to classification and dating.

plate The backplate of the two plates supporting the mechanism of a clock, or, in the plural, the front plate or dialplate and the backplate together.

pull repeat See repeating work.

push repeat See repeating work.

quarter strike Strike (chime) that tells the quarter- and half-hours as well as the hour.

rack strike or rack-and-snail strike. Mechanism to regulate the strike train by the movement of the hands, introduced c1676.

rating nut The nut and screw with which the bob (and so the rate of swing) of a pendulum can be adjusted.

regulator 18thC term for precision timepiece.

remontoire Device for rewinding the mainspring, ensuring its constant thrust.

repeating clock Clock with a repeating work.

repeating work Device in which the pull of a cord or push of a button will operate the strike (again). Invented c1676, so making it possible to hear the time in the dark.

rod Rod of the pendulum.

single-train movement Movement utilizing the same train for "going" and for striking.

Staartklok Dutch wall clock (meaning "tail clock"), c1800, with a pendulum and anchor escapement.

strike/silent ring Dial or ring with a pointer to disengage or re-engage the striking mechanism.

strut table clock Table clock provided with a strut to hold it steady, usual 19thC.

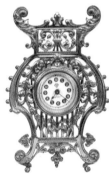

subsidiary Short for subsidiary dial.

thirty-hour Movement requiring winding every 30 hours.

three-train movement Movement with one train for "going", a second for striking the hours, and a third for an alarm or for striking the half- or quarter-hours.

two-train movement Movement with one train for "going", another for striking.

train Set of wheels, etc, locked in drive.

turret clock Clock of type installed in medieval towers, driven by a weight suspended on a rope wound round a drum. Even miniature clocks with this type of drive are called turret clocks.

verge escapement Early mechanism for regulating the movement. The verge is a rod with two bits or "pallets" that engage in the teeth of the escape wheel (the last wheel of the movement's train, also known as the "crown" wheel) and restrain it. The restraining force was provided either by a foliot or (from 17thC) by a pendulum connected to the verge. The verge escapement, though inferior to the anchor escapement, continued to be used for bracket clocks through 18thC.

vernier Sliding calibrated scale read in conjunction with the fixed scale to obtain a more accurate reading on a barometer.

Zaanklok Dutch weight-driven wall clock, 17thC. Its case extends both above and below the dial, because it houses a pendulum suspended well above the movement; it has glass sides so that the wheels, which may be decorated, can be seen. Usually there are sculpted figures above the dial.

Regions, makers & styles

Middle Eastern

Agra A main centre of rug production in India, from Mogul times (late 16thC). Designs and colours derive from Persia, but with native motifs.

Afshar Persian tribal rugs from the area south of Kirman (Kerman).

Ainabad Kurdish rugs also known as Bibikabads, from village in NW Iran.

Bakhtiara Semi-nomadic tribal rugs woven near Isfahan. Baluchistan Region covering SW Pakistan and SE Iran where rugs resembling Turkoman types are produced.

Birjand Trade name for rugs of coarse type sold through Meshed.

Caucasian Like Turkish carpets, Caucasian carpets usually have Ghiordes knots and geometric designs. In Caucasian examples, however, the geometric grid of the design is dominant, and usually includes stylized motifs. Tribal types or centres of rug production in the region include: Baku, Daghestan, Gendje, Kazakistan, Kuba, Leshgi, Shirvan, Sumak, Talish, Tchi-Tchi.

Dorukhsh (Dorosh) Fine quality 19thC carpets from Kainat area in Eastern Iran.

Heriz (Herez) Major weaving centre in NW Iran.

Isfahan Town in W. Central Iran. Great centre of art from the 16thC. Many colours used, commonly navy blue, red, beige and turquoise.

Kashan Town in central Iran, famous from 16thC for its silk carpets. In the best, silk was used in warp, weft and pile. Of all Persian carpets, Kashan are regarded as the best.

Kashgai Tribal and village rugs from Fars, S Iran, especially Fars lion rugs.

Kazak From Kazakistan in the Caucasus, a region known for its bright (fine reds and yellows) geometric designs.

Regions, makers & styles

Khorassan Generic name for carpets woven in eastern province of Iran, beware as the term is often misused.

Kirman (Kerman) Region in southern Iran, known especially for its "vase-pattern" carpets.

Kuba Region in Armenia. Caucasian type carpets, with stylized dragon motif and bright, stylized floral designs.

Kum City in central Iran with important modern weaving industry, known for its calli-graphic (Kufic) designs.

Kurdish Generic name for tribal weaving from NW Iran.

Malayer Fine Kurdish-type weaving from village near Arak.

Mehreban Area near Heriz; sometimes a particular quality of rug.

Persian Persian rugs have great variety of design and colour, attributable to the influence from other arts and from China that revolution-ized rug-making in 16thC Iran. They may feature an arabesque, geometric or floral pattern, or incorporate natura-listic motifs, eg horsemen. Specifically "Persian" is a design based on a central medallion surrounded by dense stylized floral motifs. Centres of rug production or tribal types include: Bakhtiara, Bidjar, Fereghan, Hamadan, Herat, Heriz, Isfahan, Kashan, Kashgai, Kirman, Kum, Meshed, Nain, Saruk, Sehna, Shiraz, Tabriz.

Polonaise Silk carpet of a type evolved in Isfahan in Iran in 16thC but also made in Kashan, with a symmetrical floral design in soft, almost pastel colours, enhanced by gold and silver brocade. Carpets of this type were found in the collection of a Polish prince and this gave rise to term "polonaise" in 19thC.

Qum see Kum.

Saraband Term applied to rugs woven in and around the town of Arak in Iran.

Serab (Sarab) Rugs from a village of the same name near Heriz in Iran.

Shirvan Rugs from Shirvan in the Caucasus; also known as "Baku" or "Kabistan". Appreciated for their fine, short pile, they have a wide range of decoration, extending to motifs generally associated with Persian rugs.

Sumak (Soumak) Region of the Caucasus, known for its flat-woven carpets or "kelim", which are often decorated with a running pattern in the weft. Unlike other kelim, Sumak carpets are usable one side up only.

Regions, makers & styles

Tabriz Town in NW Iran, the original capital of the Persian Safavid dynasty (1502-1736). Typically its carpets are designed round one, or several, medallions, while the ground is filled with a dense multitude of floral "shoots".

Turkish Also known as "Anatolian" carpets. Like Caucasian carpets, Turkish rugs usually have a geometric design, for example a repeating arabesque, which produces an overall pattern. If the design is more structured, its elements are simple (for example a "mihrab") and recognisable motifs are few. Turkish types or centres of rug production include: Bergama, Ghiordes, Karabagh, Kirsehir, Ladik, Milas, Ushak, Yuruk.

Turkoman Carpets from western Turkestan. Made by nomads or semi-nomads, usually with a Sehna knot. Show a limited repertoire of geometric patterns, dominated by a repeating "gul" or stylized flower. Famed for their soothing, subtle colours. Turkoman tribes include: Salor, Tekke, Yomud.

Other regions and makers

Aubusson Town in France, where tapestries, coverings and carpets have been produced since 17thC. The carpets have a tapestry-weave (that is, they do not have a knotted pile) and are known for their large floral designs.

Axminster Town in Devon, England, where moquette or pileless carpets were made from mid 18thC till 1835, when the factory was moved to Wilton. At Wilton, "Axminster" mechanically woven carpets continue to be made today.

Gobelins Name of the French royal factory mainly producing tapestries for the king from 18thC.

Sprague, W.P. A carpet factory in Philadelphia, Pennsylvania, US, which made finger-tufted rugs at end of 18thC.

Wilton Town in Wiltshire, England, where there has been a carpet factory since c1740. At first used a moquette weave, Wilton switched to knotted carpets in 19thC, and also mechanized the process.

Introduction

- The most important factor is country of origin, and where the rug was made there. Also consider age, condition, rarity, demand, quality and design.

- Top of the scale are fine silk rugs from Persia and Turkey. Quality wool rugs from Persia and the Caucasus command high prices. Modern rugs and those from other areas are relatively less expensive but no rug, of reasonable quality, condition and pedigree, will be cheap.

- In general, the older the rug the greater its investment potential. "Antique" rugs, over 100 years old, command the highest prices; "old" rugs, over 50 years old, are sought after.

- Next in importance is richness and harmony of colour, fineness and the interest of the design, and the patina which dyed fibres acquire with age.

- A hand-made rug has the pattern visible on the back of the surface. Part pile and look for rows of knots at base of tuft. Absence of either indicates a machine-made rug of little interest.

- Rugs of synthetically-dyed fibres, are often garish and weak. Chemical dye comes off on a damp white handkerchief, and has an unpleasant smell. Some vegetable dyes will also leave a stain, but slight by comparison.

- The back of an old rug will have a polished appearance and flattened knots.

- Check tufts with a magnifying glass. In old rugs the colour should shade gradually from deep at the base to pale at the tip. Three bands of colour indicates a newer rug artificially aged.

- Never buy a rug that has been attacked by mildew. Signs are pale patches on the back and rotten fibres which snap when rug is folded or twisted.

- Check rugs for holes and wear by holding up to a strong light. Weak areas can be strengthened and repaired if not too extensive, but cost of repair should be reflected in price.

- Repairs can be detected with the palm of the hand as raised or uneven areas of pile. A skilfull repair using correctly matched colours and vegetable dye will not substantially affect value.

- Top prices should only be paid for complete rugs. Many have had worn areas removed. Check the pattern and borders.

- Fringes are especially vulnerable to wear and removal. It is better to buy a rug with a replaced fringe than one in which the fringe has been removed and a new one made by fraying the edges of the rug.

- Dates (in arabic characters) woven into the rug can be misleading.

Glossary

abadeh Strong, highly coloured Persian rug, with design usually including tree-of-life and diamond-shaped medallion.

abrash Oriental carpets made by nomads are especially subject to variation within a colour; this is termed "abrash".

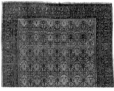

abrisham Persian silk. allover rug with an allover, repeating pattern.

aniline dye Industrial dye. Aniline dyes, introduced into Oriental carpet manufacture c1870, are considered much inferior to the traditional vegetable dyes.

baff A knot.

boteh Type of motif, essentially a leaf form, but curled at the tip, inspired European Paisley pattern.

candy Side cord of rug.

chain Term sometimes used for the threads of the warp or weft.

chrome dye Modern industrial dye now used widely in the East, faster and more stable than anilines.

corridor carpet Long thin carpet, also known as a "runner".

dhurri Indian equivalent of kelim (q.v.).

doruye Rug with different design on each side; reversible.

dragon-lung Male dragon symbol on Chinese rugs.

feng-huang Chinese female dragon-phoenix symbol, opposite of dragon-lung.

field Area of a carpet within its borders.

flat or **flat-woven carpet** Carpet without a pile; see also kilim.

Ghiordes knot Type of pile, also called "Turkish". The "knot" is formed by passing a thread round two "chains" of the warp and through the space between.

guard stripe Stripe immediately surrounding the field of the Persian carpet, even inside the inner stripe.

gul Persian word for "flower"; the stylized geometric pattern, concentric like a flower, that recurs in many variations, particularly on Turkoman carpets.

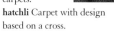

hatchli Carpet with design based on a cross.

herati pattern Design common on Persian rugs. It has a repeating unit consisting of several elements, usually floral ones, arranged in two- or four-way symmetry round a centre, typically a rosette.

Kashmir Area in northern India producing silk and wool rugs.

kilim (ghilim, khilim) Rugs without a "knot" or "pile"; also known as "flat" carpets.

mihrab Hollow or niche in the wall of a mosque that faces towards Mecca; often adopted as a structural element of the design particularly in Turkish rugs.

mir Persian rug with palm-leaf motifs.

mira Palm-leaf motif.

moquette Heavy imitation velvet, used for upholstery; also used as an alternative to knotting to produce an apparent pile, eg on Axminster carpets.

motif Item or element of a design, whether geometric, stylized or naturalistic.

mud Finely-woven rugs made in area around Khorassan in Iran, with geometric designs.

mudjur Turkish prayer mat, usually of wool.

namas Rug on which to pray, typically not more than 3ft (91cm) long, and a little less wide.

nomad rugs Rugs woven by wandering central Asian tribes, never entirely symmetrical and usually with a fringe at each end.

pendant Smaller design element usually attached on each side of a medallion.

pile Short pieces of thread or yarn "knotted" to the warp and weft of a carpet, constituting its upper surface.

pillar rug Chinese rug so made that it can be arranged round a pillar.

prayer rug Rug on which a Muslim normally kneels when he prays. It is personal and precious, so often finely worked, but invariably small. Frequently it incorporates a mihrab design.

savonnerie French rug in the Oriental style, with cut pile. From 17thC.

Sehna (Senneh, Sinneh) Type of pile, also called "Persian". The "knot" is formed by passing a thread round two "chains" of the warp and out beside the second.

Folk Art

- Europe has a heritage of Folk Art. The techniques and styles were taken to the US by 18thC and 19thC immigrants.
- Local woods such as pine, maple or cherry were used to make simple furniture and boxes which were then brightly painted.
- Painting on furniture and on ceramics tends to be simple and stylized. Motifs derived from nature, especially tulips, hearts and birds, popular.
- Blanket chests might be painted with panels of formalized folk imagery. Those made c1750-c1850 may feature initials and dates.

A 19thC carved and painted pine standing eaglet.

- Itinerant craftsmen made hand-carved and painted ornaments and homewares.
- Tinware is usually simply made, coffee pots being common. Painted examples are often decorated with "gaudy" tulips.
- Pottery is typically redware, much remains from late 18thC on.

- Illuminated manuscripts known by German word fraktur record births or a family tree. Best examples feature vivid imagery and bold colours. Early (pre-1790) dates not uncommon.

A painted and decorated oval bentwood ribbon box. c1800

- Bed quilts were made in large numbers from the 18thC and have often been well preserved. Other textiles include hooked rugs, the best examples feature bold stylized designs.
- Samplers were commonly pictorial, featured alphabets, "improving" or religious texts, or personal details. Collectors usually pay a premium for pictorial examples while religious ones tend to be less valuable. Conditon is important.

A needlework sampler signed "Jane Halsey March 10 1825".

A 17thC Scandinavian burr wood peg tankard.

- common decoration.
- Examples from late 17thC can be difficult to distinguish from later reproductions.
- 18thC treen drinking vessels and other utensils are often finely turned and in a variety of woods: maple, walnut, mahogany and lignum vitae.
- Such 18thC pieces are sought after, but the collector has to be on guard against late Victorian reproductions.

- The term "Treen" is used to describe small wooden objects normally associated with everyday domestic, trade, professional or rural life.
- Most pieces have been turned on a lathe and are not normally the work of a cabinet-maker or joiner. Items tend to be smaller than a spinning wheel.
- Carving, poker-work, inlay and painting are

A 18thC North American burlwood boat-shaped bowl.

These tend to be of poorer quality mahogany and are generally cruder and less elegant in execution.
- Patination should be present, but faking is not unknown.
- Fine carving, especially if combined with skilful turning and attractive graining, adds greatly to value. Mottoes and quotations, carved or in poker-work, are also desirable, but beware later additions to genuine but plain items.

An 18thC French carved coquilla nut snuff box.

Boxes

MAUCHLINEWARE

Produced from the early 19thC until 1933, in the Scottish town, Mauchline in Ayrshire.

- Souvenir ware. Produced primarily by W. & A. Smith.
- Sycamore wood decorated with dark 'decal' applied as transfer.
- Predominantly boxes, also napkin rings, rulers, photo frames etc.

PENWORK

Penwork was used to decorate japanned items in the late 18thC and early 19thC, mainly in England.

- Delicate lacy effect, like etching in reverse.
- White motifs on black ground.
- First japanned black, then pattern painted on in white japan, then details/shading added in black.

POKER WORK

Technique involving application of a heated instrument such as a poker to wood, creating decoration and dimension.

- Practiced by the ancient Egyptians, revived in 19thC.
- Often on sycamore/beech/birch.
- Also known as 'woodburning' or 'pyrography'.

QUILLWORK

Perhaps the oldest form of embroidery used by Native Americans.

- Porcupine quills were dyed, then folded, twisted, wrapped, plaited and sewn onto a variety of items using a wide range of techniques.
- Used to decorate articles of clothing, bags, boxes, etc.

ROLLED PAPERWORK

Sometimes called paper filigree or
paper quilling, this technique
involves strips of paper wound
around a quill to create basic coils,
then glued at the tip and arranged to
form decorative designs.

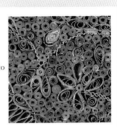

- Used on high quality boxes and
  caddies, but also practised by
  young ladies of the early 19thC.

PAINTED PAPIER MÂCHÉ

Introduced to England by mid-late
17thC. Became popular by 19thC.

- Made from pulped paper, glue,
  chalk, sometimes sand. Often
  embellished with mother-of-
  pearl. Mainly small objects.
- Notably, finely painted boxes by
  German manufacturer, Johann
  Heinrich Stobwasser (1740-1829).

TARTANWARE

Tartanware refers to small wooden
objects covered in a tartan pattern.

- Scottish souvenir ware.
- Dates from the early 1850s
  onwards when colour-printed
  paper was glued to the piece, then
  lightly varnished.
- Often invented different tartans.
- Predominantly boxes.

Prince Charlie

TUNBRIDGEWARE

Produced as souvenir ware in
Tunbridge Wells, UK, from 17thC.

- Most pieces available to collectors
  date from mid-late 19thC.
- 'Stickwork' – slim rods of wood
  stuck together, then sliced hori-
  zontally to form 'mosaic' design.
- Boxes, rulers and frames typical.

Antiquities

A 4thC Roman glass flask with two handles and dimpled body.

- Antiquities are fragile and susceptible to corrosion. Any cleaning should be undertaken by experts.
- Watch out for forgeries, especially of ancient glass, Roman coins and erotic Samian bowls and lamps.

- Objects made before AD600 in Europe, and pre-Columbian in US, are generally classed as antiquities.
- Most countries have laws governing the excavation and export of antiquities. Objects legitimately on the market come from 18thC and 19thC collections. Nevertheless there is much robbed material.
- Buy well documented pieces from reputable dealers, with an export licence and museum certificate of authenticity.

- Collectors will pay good prices for rare pieces, or works of artistic merit, even if in fragmentary condition. Vice versa, the commoner an object is, the more condition is important.

A Late Period Egyptian turquoise faience Ushabti.

An Italian brick red ware urn, painted with figures.

- Marriages are also quite common; genuine ancient glass or ceramic fragments are made up into vessels, but rarely to a known and recorded shape.
- Reproductions also confuse the collector. Pieces that were made for museum shops can be passed off as genuine.

Netsuke

- Netsuke are Japanese carved toggles, originally made to secure a portable medicine box (inro) or similar item, which hung from the waist on a cord. Usually made of wood or ivory, they date from about 16thC.
- There is keen competition for signed netsuke by masters of the art, as well as those depicting rare or novel subjects. Otherwise, netsuke can be collected fairly inexpensively, but avoid incompetent workmanship, dull subjects, damaged pieces or early 20thC copies. The best pieces are hand-carved.

A mid-19thC ivory netsuke of a grimacing face with horns.

genuine period ornaments (okimono), converted to netsuke by boring a cord hole. In genuine netsuke, the hole is designed to be almost invisible; in fakes the holes are often clumsily obtrusive.

- Recent copies lack patina. The grain in genuine ivory is only visible at certain angles, whereas simulated ivory grain is visible and very regular. Signatures on fakes are often moulded, not carved.

A 19thC carved wood netsuke of a recumbent cow.

- Ivory is not necessarily more valuable than wood, especially since ivory netsuke were mass-produced for export in the late 19thC. However, inlaid netsuke often command a premium.
- Copies and fakes are numerous. Some are

An ivory okimono of two entertainers. c1870

Perfume bottles

- Perfume bottles display every technique of the glass maker's art and are collected for their novel shapes, colours and decoration. Today, commercial bottles are also collected and can be valuable.
- The best buys are 18thC coloured glass bottles, decorated with gilt and enamel with silver or gold caps; later 18thC James

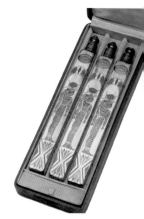

An Ahmed Soliman set of crystal perfume bottles. 1920s

A Hoffman perfume bottle, with jewelled decoration. 1920s

Giles bottles, faceted and gilded on opaque white glass; and Art Deco bottles designed by Daum, Gallé and Lalique.
- Porcelain bottles made at Chelsea, Bow and Worcester in the late 18thC are also desirable, many

modelled in the shape of human or animal figures; particularly collectable are the bottles from the Girl in a Swing factory. 19thC forgeries exist which are hard to distinguish from the originals.
- 20thC bottles made for manufacturers such as Schiaparelli, Chanel, Nina Ricci and Avon are all collectable. Limited edition examples command a premium.

A double ended cranberry glass scent bottle. c1870

Sewing accessories

A British silver souvenir thimble. 1920s-30s

- Sewing tools have been produced for centuries, but the majority of those on the market today date from the late 18thC and particualrly the 19thC.
- Many of the small items were originally part of the complete, fitted sewing boxes owned by most wealthy 19thC women.
- Tools were made from wood, mother of pearl, silver, brass, glass and even gold.
- Look for thimbles and thimble cases, needlecases (including averys – pressed brass cases designed to hold different sized needles), pin cushions, thread winders, scissors, tape measures and sewing compendia.
- As a general rule, the price of thimbles reflects the intrinsic value of the material and the fineness of the decoration.
- Gold thimbles are rare and even plain examples are costly. Silver thimbles are next in value, followed by

the base metals. Hand-painted enamel and porcelain have a high value for their rarity, whereas prices for other materials, such as ivory, tortoiseshell, mother of pearl and glass depend upon quality.

- Trademarks and advertising slogans can increase the value of base metal thimbles, but most sought-after are patented types: the Dorcas ventilated thimble, the non-slip, and those with a needle-threader or cutter attached.
- Thimble cases are worth more with the original thimble inside. Look especially for pre-1850 silver, gold, enamel, hardwood and leather examples and for cases with needle compartments and novel shapes.
- Beware of modern silver thimbles which lack patina but resemble 18thC and 19thC originals.

A Spanish walnut sewing compendium. c1850

Figurines

- With any figurine, you should consider the form, the maker, designer, and the material.

- Elegant Art Deco figurines are currently particularly popular. These are often mounted on a marble base called a socle. Most figurines were in the shape of graceful and fashionable young women. These were frequently dancers, athletes, or in some way inspired by the jazz movement.

- Most Art Deco figures are either ceramic, bronze or chryselephantine (a combination of bronze and ivory). In general, the latter will be worth more. Fakes and reproductions are very common, so check that ivory is not ivorene or plastic by looking closely for the characteristic lines of ivory. The works of designers like Ferdinand Preiss and Demêtre Chiparus are extremely desirable.

- Some of the most desirable Art Deco ceramic figures were made by the Austrian manufacturer,

A Ferdinand Preiss Champagne Dancer bronze and ivory figure. c1930

A pair Stefan Dakon female dancers by Goldscheider. c1940

Goldscheider, who produced faithful copies of modern couture. Their pieces, often designed by Stefon Dakon or Josef Lorenzl, exhibit meticulous attention to complex moulded details.

A Josef Lorenzl patinated bronze dancer. 1920s

A Royal Dux figure group of a courting couple, by Hampel.

of a particular designer, eg Leslie Harradine. When buying a Royal Doulton figurine, you should also consider the colour as a figure may have been produced in several different colourways. Each variation has an allocated 'HN' number and is likely to be worth a different amount, depending on rarity. Pre-WWI figurines, and later lines that were a limited edition or cancelled quickly due to unpopularity are now rare and more desirable.

■ Look for damage at the base and the

■ With other mass-produced figurines, be sure to consider quality of moulding and painting. Rarity is also important and hence consider how long the figure was in production.

■ One of the most prolific manufacturers of figurines is Royal Doulton, which has produced over 4,000 different models and colour variations. Many collectors choose to collect a type, eg the 'Fair Ladies', children or literary and historical characters, or the work

A Royal Doulton Top O' The Hill figurine. Introduced 1937.

extremities. Mass-produced figurines, like those these, are widely available, and so damage will affect value considerably.

A Lenci figure of a fashionably dressed skier. 1930s

Bisque dolls

A Steiner B doll, lever eyed, with open mouth. c1880

and more realistic painting, even on identical models, will usually increase value.

- Pleasantly expressive faces, like those produced by the French manufacturer Jumeau, are particularly desirable and valuable.
- Look out for character dolls, which have highly expressive faces (laughing or crying), or that are dressed as characters, as these can be valuable.
  - Many eyes are 'sleeping' and are weighted so that they close when the doll is laid down. 'Flirty' eyes moving from side to side are scarcer.

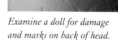

Examine a doll for damage and marks on back of head.

- When looking at any bisque doll, consider the same factors. Begin by examining all parts of the doll, from head to toe.
- Well-modelled heads are more desirable. Finer

- An open mouth, which may contain teeth, can also add to the appeal of a doll. This feature was used from c1890.
- The head is typically worth about 50% of the overall value, so should be examined closely.
- Bisque should be smooth

Look for well painted and well moulded, expressive features.

Bisque dolls

The more articulated limbs a doll has, the higher the value.

and clean. Any damage (such as cracks and chips) will reduce value considerably. Shining a strong light inside the head will cause cracks to show up as lines. Always ask the owner before carefully removing the wig to do this.

- The back of the head may also have incised or impressed marks. These may include the mould number, and the maker's name or motif. The mould number can often help to identify the maker.
- An original wig is also desirable, but a wig that is correct for that doll is acceptable. Wigs that have been cut or dyed should be avoided.
- In general, larger dolls are more valuable, though some miniature dolls are very collectable.
- The body should be original, though it may not have been made by the same manufacturer as the head.
- Dolls made from different, assembled parts will have a lower value.
- Generally, the more articulated joints a body has, the higher quality it is.
- Loose or detached, but undamaged limbs, can be restrung by a doll-restorer, so this should not affect the price too greatly.
- Look closely at thumbs and fingers as they are vulnerable to damage.
- Original, period clothes should always be retained, even if shabby. Dolls dressed in clothes

Original or period clothes such as these shoes can add value.

made by the manufacturer are preferable, but this is rare.
- Generally, appropriate period clothing is accepted as standard.
- Good quality period doll clothes and shoes can also command a reasonable price, even without an accompanying doll.

Bisque doll manufacturers

- The golden age of bisque doll production lasted from the mid-19thC to the 1930s. The major makers were based in France and Thuringia in Germany.
- In general, German dolls were less expensive than

Initials and star on a Kammer & Reinhardt doll's head.

Marks on the back of a black doll by Ernst Heubach.

French dolls, but they were still well made and extremely popular.

- Ernst Heubach, based in Koppelsdorf, Germany, produced dolls from 1887. The firm merged with Armand Marseille in 1919, and split once again in 1932. Between these dates, dolls were marked 'Heubach Koppelsdorf'.
- Jumeau was founded by Pierre François Jumeau in France, c1842. Its dolls are

Printed marks on the back of a doll's head by Jumeau.

highly regarded for their beautiful faces and couture dresses.

- Character dolls, such as the sad 'Jumeau Triste' dolls, are highly sought after.
- The company won the Gold Medal at the Paris Exhibition in 1878 and this was advertised on doll's bodies, boxes and labels.
- Printed red marks are the most common, with 'E.J.' marks and a size number being earlier.
- Armand Marseille was

Incised marks on the back of an Armand Marseille 390 doll.

founded in Germany in 1885, and grew to be one of the most prolific producers, active until the 1920s.

- The company produced the '390' doll, which is the most commonly found period bisque doll.
- Kämmer & Reinhardt was founded in 1886 in Germany. Most of its heads were made by Simon & Halbig. The

Bisque doll manufacturers

company claimed to be responsible for introducing character dolls from 1909, as well as dolls with bisque teeth.

- Max Handwerck was a German doll maker active from c1900 onwards.
- Goebel produced many

Impressed marks on the back of a Max Handwerck doll's head.

of its heads, and often used the tradenames 'Bébé Elite' or 'Triumph Bébé'. Dolls marked 'Handwerck' only are by another company Heinrich Handwerck.

- Simon and Halbig was founded in Germany in 1839 and began doll

Impressed marks on the back of a doll's head by Simon & Halbig

production in the late 1860s. As well as making its own dolls, it made heads for other companies including Jumeau, S.F.B.J., and Kämmer & Reinhardt, which bought the company in 1920. The '&' mark between the two names was added in 1905.

- Bru was founded in France in 1866 and produced very fine quality dolls until 1899, when it became part of S.F.B.J.
- Fakes and reproductions are common. Look for pierced earlobes, gracefully curving arms and the presence of mould numbers near the 'Bru Jne' company name.
- S.F.B.J. (Société Français de Fabrication des Bébés et Jouets) was a group of French doll makers who joined forces from 1899

Impressed marks on the back of a French doll's head by S.F. B.J.

to c1950 to challenge the dominance of the German industry. It included Jumeau and Bru. They produced both bébé and character dolls. Quality varies widely.

- Steiner was founded by Jules Steiner in 1855 in France. Its dolls were of fine quality, using a pale bisque. Some are marked 'Bourgoin', who was a retailer associated with Steiner during the 1880s.

Types of dolls

WOODEN

Wooden dolls known as 'babies' became more common during the 16th and 17thC.

■ Made on lathes, often by chairmakers and sold at fairs or made at home. Clothes often homemade.

■ Early 17thC: tapered waist. Late 17thC: no waist, and often crudely carved.

PORCELAIN

First produced in Thuringia, Germany, were most popular from c1840-c1880.

■ Most made in Germany or France.

■ French dolls more refined than German. Swivel heads, handmade costumes. Often real hair.

■ 'Parian' became generic name for fine half-vitreous porcelain. Most made in Germany c1870-1900.

FABRIC

Though cloth dolls have been popular from earliest times, they were often thrown away so, for the collector, the first significant examples date from the 19thC. Mass production started c1830.

■ US: Izannah Walker, Rhode Island (active 1880s-1925). Oil-painted features, stitched hands with separate thumbs.

■ German: Kämmer & Reinhardt the first to make safe, washable dolls. Käthe Kruse made washable dolls from 1912.

■ Britain: Chad Valley, notable for models based on princesses Elizabeth and Margaret. Norah Wellings left Chad Valley in 1926 to form her own company, which made dolls with velvet/felt heads.

■ Italy: Lenci, founded in Turin 1918 by Enrico di Scavini. Sophisticated dolls intended for adults. Between c1920-1940 vast range of dolls in elaborate costumes produced.

■ Must be in good condition/clean as many cannot be washed.

Types of dolls

WAX

Pressed-wax dolls with moulded or carved solid heads were made until the 1840s, when British dollmakers began making poured wax dolls.

- Henry Pierotti (1809-71), London, invented first baby dolls. Sweet faces, blue eyes.
- Augusta Montanari (1818-64), London. Elaborate costumes, heavy shoulders, despairing expression.

COMPOSITION

Used as an inexpensive alternative to bisque and china in the 19thC and 20thC.

- Wood and paper pulp strengthened with rags, bones, eggs (in Europe); wood, plastic (US).
- Led by Germany pre-WW1. After: led by USA.
- US makers developed collectable range, including Shirley Temple.

HARD PLASTIC

Hard plastic was used to make dolls from 1945 until the 1950s.

- Inexpensive and durable.
- Alexander Doll Co., New York, US. Huge range of named dolls, including the "Little Women" series.

- British companies: Rosebud (merged with Mattel 1967), Pedigree, British National Dolls Ltd.
- Mint boxed condition preferable.

VINYL (SOFT PLASTIC)

Hard plastic dolls superseded by vinyl, which was softer to the touch, in 1950s.

- 1959: Barbie launched by Mattel. Pre-1961 most sought after. Date by hairstyle. Brunette/red-headed dolls rare.
  - 1962: launch of UK rival, Sindy, by Pedigree.
  - Mint boxed condition essential.

Glossary

autoperipatetikos Greek for "walking about by itself", the common term for 19thC clockwork dolls.

baby house A dolls' house. These survive from 17thC.

ball-jointed With limbs that move by swivelling on a ball, as opposed to "stiff-jointed".

bébé French doll, modelled as a child about 8–12 years old. Made by Bru and others in second half 19thC.

bent-limb Doll made only to sit, with limbs fixed in bent position.

bisque Made of biscuit pottery, eg doll with bisque head, all-bisque doll.

blonde bisque Term for early bisque dolls tinted slightly pink.

character doll Similar to a portrait doll, but not representing anyone specifically; has a naturalistic physiognomy.

composition doll Doll made of cheap materials such as wood pulp, paper pulp and size.

estate-made Made on the estate of a great house by a staff craftsman, as was common 17thC–19thC.

Frozen Charlotte Doll made of china that could be used in the bath, Germany, 19thC.

googlie eyes Eyes that can be moved, eg by means of a string in the back of the head. From first years of 20thC.

gutta-percha Not to be confused with rubber, but similar to it, a synthetic substance used for making dolls in second half 19thC.

intaglio eyes Eyes modelled by incising into the bisque.

marotte Type of poupard that plays a tune when spun round.

open-closed mouth Doll's mouth modelled in such a way as to appear open.

paperweight eyes Glass eyes coloured using the same technique as for marbles or paperweights.

parian Stoneware developed in 19thC and good for modelling eg dolls' heads; loosely, any bisque doll that is not painted.

Parisienne French doll, made from 1860s to 1880s by makers such as Jumeau or Rohmer, having a bisque head and usually a kid-leather body.

pate Crown of a doll's head, beneath the wig if it has one. Can be made in a variety of materials depending on the maker. In better dolls, usually of cork.

portrait doll Doll modelled to represent somebody well known.

poupard Doll without a lower body but set instead on a stick, which is usually covered by the doll's clothes.

poured wax Dolls moulded in wax.

Pouty Character doll with a pouting expression, of which Kammer and Reinhardt's model 117 is a famous example.

printed doll Rag doll with fabric covering on which facial and body features were printed.

Queen Anne doll Carved and jointed wooden doll of fixed facial type made in 18thC.

rooted hair Hair not moulded, but in tufts, in the wax scalp.

shoulder head Doll's head made in one piece with neck and collar, and inserted into body.

stump doll Doll made of a single piece of wood, without joints.

three-faced Like a two-faced doll, but with three. A speciality of Carl Bergner.

turnabout Rag doll with two different faces, one of which would, at any one time, be covered by a bonnet.

turnover doll Rag doll made with two different heads, one of which would he covered by the reversible skirt.

two-faced Doll with a revolving head, able to show a choice of two faces.

voice box Device by which the doll can talk, cry, etc.

waxed Composition doll dipped in wax to give a surface finish.

Teddy bears

A 1920s Steiff bear, note the long arms, pronounced snout.

as the smell of use cannot be faked.

- The type of fabric should help date the bear. Vintage bears are usually made from wool mohair, whilst artificial silk plush was used from c1930. During WWII materials were eclectic, based on what could be acquired. Synthetic fabrics were introduced in the 1950s.

- Pre-war bears are the most collectable, though due to the rarity of bears of this type, post-war bears by good makers are rising in value.
- Fakes are commonplace, as are legitimate reproductions by major makers.
- Bears that are too 'well loved' with worn fur are less desirable, but most old bears should have some form of wear consistent with play (eg on back/snout, dragged arms). Smell your bear,

Examine features such as noses as they can provide clues.

The form of a head can often help identify a maker and date.

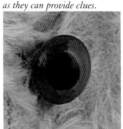

Eyes may be replaced. Glass was used from the 1930s.

- When determining the manufacturer, look at the general shape of bear and, in particular, its head as these are often particular.

Teddy bears

Boot button eyes were the earliest form of eye used.

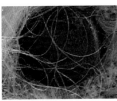

An early Steiff blank button, used from 1905-09.

A Steiff button with an under-scored 'f', used 1905-1950s.

- Older bears tend to have longer snouts and limbs, whatever their manufacturer. The shape of the nose can also be revealing, as somes manufacturers had their own distinct style at certain times.

- The eyes should be appropriate to the period. Except in Britain (where they were used as early as 1912), glass eyes only became widely used in the 1920s, so most pre-WWI bears should have boot button eyes. Plastic eyes were used from the 1950s.

- The label is obviously the easiest way of identifying the maker. Even if the label is missing, it is worth looking for evidence of its position on the bear as this varies. Stieff, for example, are well known for their Button-in-the-Ear trademark, which was patented in 1905.

MINIATURE BEARS

Miniature bears were most famously made by Schuco (Schreyer & Co.) and Stieff from the 1920s onwards.

- Typically no paw pads (except Schuco 1920s bears).

- Many Schuco bears tinplate covered in mohair: combination exclusive to Schuco.

- Schuco novelty bears conceal perfume bottles, compacts etc. Mechanical bears. Rare colours like bright orange/purple most desirable. 'Berlin bear' with crown and sash.

- Schuco sold in 1970s. Stieff still producing miniature bears.

A Schuco peach mohair miniature bear.

Teddy bear makers

CHAD VALLEY

Founded in England in 1820, first teddy bears produced 1915, taken over by Palitoy in 1978.

- Rounded heads with large, flat ears.
- 1920s-30s: tin-plate buttons used.
- 1930s: stitched label. 1950s: printed 'Hygienic' toys fabric label.
- 1938-53: Royal Warrant foot label. Post 1953 "Queen Mother" label.

CHILTERN

Founded in England in 1908, first bears produced 1915, taken over by Chad Valley 1967.

- 'Chiltern Toys' name used from 1924.
- 1920s-30s bears have shaved muzzles and two vertical nose stitches.
- 1920s-60s: popular 'Hugmee' range.
- Post war bears have shorter limbs and plumper bodies.

FARNELL

Established in London 1897, first bears produced 1921, closed 1968.

- Known as 'English Steiff' due to shape and high quality.
- 'Alpha' trademark registered in 1925.
- Pre-war bears feature long arms, shaved muzzle, vertical nose stitching, large ears, plump body, back hump, cardboard inserts in feet.

AMERICAN BEARS

Majors makers include Ideal (est.1903), Knickerbocker (bears c1920-80s), Bruin (1907-09) and Hecla (c1907-c1915)

- Arms typically low on body, ears wide apart on triangular head, pointed feet. Steiff-style shape.
- Numerous short-lived makers, most bears unmarked.

Teddy bear makers

MERRYTHOUGHT

Founded in England in 1930.

- 1930-45: Metal or celluloid button. 1945-56: 'Hygienic Toys' label. 1957-91: 'Iron Bridge, Shrops' printed label.
- Until 1950s: nose stitched vertically, two vertical stitches beneath.
- Factory still active today.

SCHUCO (SCHREYER & CO.)

Founded Germany 1912, sold in 1970s.

- 'Yes/No' bears with moving head and tail introduced 1921.
- Well-known for range of miniature bears produced 1920s-50s with hidden features including compacts and perfume bottles.
- Colours such as green, purple and orange rare and desirable.

STEIFF

Founded Germany 1877, first bears made 1902.

- Pre-WWII: long limbs, curved paws, pronounced muzzle, black boot-button eyes, humped back and expressive faces.
- Post 1951: plumper with rounder heads and shorter limbs.
- Metal button in ear can help with dating. Elephant button 1904-05, blank button 1905-09 or 1948-50, elongated and curving second 'f' of Steiff 1905-50, script wording introduced 1952.
- Many pre-war forms and models being re-released today. Look at condition, label and button.
- White bears had light-brown stitched nose. White and particularly black bears rare, cinnamon is scarce.
- A seam running down the centre of the head appeared in one in seven bears.
- Company still active today.

Toys

- Tin-plated steel super-seded wood and other metals as the primary material for making toys in the

A large Märklin limousine, with clockwork mechanism.

mid to late 19thC. It was less expensive to produce, more versatile and easy to decorate.

- 19thC tinplate tends to be hand-painted. The more cost effective colour transfer-printed lithography took over in c1900. Look out for a slightly uneven surface and brush strokes that indicate the more valuable hand-painting. Lithographed surfaces tend to be uniformly flat and shinier.

- Trains were at first crude and powered by clock-

work or steam, but by 1920 were accurate scale models of the real thing. Collectors look for early Märklin (founded 1856), Bing (1863-1933), and Hornby (parent company, Meccano, founded 1907) models.

- The most desirable tinplate models are large, complex ones such as cars, boats or trains produced pre-WWI by important German manufactures like Märklin, Bing, Lehmann (founded 1881), Carette (1886-1917), and Tipp & Co. (1912-71).

- Tiny tinplate penny toys, sold on late 19thC and early 20thC street corners for one penny, are also desirable. Condition is very important, with mint examples commanding a premium. Novelty toys and transport toys, particularly cars, planes and zepplins,

A Hornby Series electric LNER 0-4-0 Locomotive.

A Dinky No. 902 Foden Flat Truck, with box. 1954-57

are the most desirable.
- Handle as much tinplate as possible to learn how to recognise fakes. Beware of rust and scratched lithography as this is almost impossible to restore.
- Crude lead cast models were produced from the early 20thC, but after WWI, casting techniques improved as did the quality of die-cast models. As with tin-plate toys, models of cars, planes and boats are desirable.
- Consider the shape and the date of a model, and check the colour against reference books, as some are rarer and more valuable than others.
- Particularly collectable makers include Dinky (founded 1931 as Modelled Miniatures), Corgi

(founded 1956), Tootsie toys (founded 1922) and Hot Wheels (founded 1968).
- Complete sets are most sought after, especially when boxed.
- Models and boxes should be in excellent condition.
- The taste for cast iron moneyboxes with mechanical parts worked by a coin, like those produced by J. & E. Stevens (1842-1930s), has spread beyond the US. As a result, reproductions and crudely painted, poorly finished fakes are now common.

A Stevens Teddy and The Bear cast iron mechanical bank.

Toys & games

- Early die-cast lead soldiers were flat or semi-flat until Britains's hollow-cast technique led to more realistic figures from 1900. Other notable companies include Lucotte and Charbens.

- Examples with oval bases and paper labels in their original box fetch the best prices.

- After WWI, soldiers became less appealing to buyers, and so companies began to focus on civilian scenes, such as farms and circuses.

- The use of lead in children's toys was banned in 1966.

- Rocking horses continue to be popular. Early homemade 19thC American horses are most desirable. However, commercially-made British models by makers like R.H. Ayres, Collinson and Lines Brothers are a good buy.

- Other 19thC toys like jigsaws, Noah's arks and novelty balls made of interlocking parts are still

A boxed Britains Set 2092, The Parachute Regiment.

collectable, but are unlikely to quickly increase in value.

- Lead figures should never be repainted no matter how worn they are as this lowers value. Repainting can also hide repairs.

- Check heads and other extremities, such as guns, for breakage.

- Prices depend on quality of decoration, condition, age and size.

- 1950s and '60s battery-powered toys made in Japan are becoming increasingly desirable.

A battery-operated tinplate Nomura Mini Robo Tank toy.

A Star Wars 'Luke Skywalker' carded action figure. 1978

- Action figures will be more valuable if they are early and carded. It also depends on which variation of the figure you have.
- Star Wars action figures, made by Kenner in the US and Palitoy in the UK from 1977, are the most desirable. Star Trek figures produced by Mego are becoming more valuable.
- The earliest Luke Skywalker figure with the telescoping lightsabre is the most valuable for that character.
- Toys with a history linking them to an owner, particularly the aristocratic or famous, are much sought after.

Large robots are particularly valuable. A 'mystery action' (eg movement, lights), will add value.

CHESS

Chess uses rules set down in 15thC Italy, though similar games have been played since the second century BC.

- Chess became very popular in the 18thC and 19thC when many sets made. Earlier examples, rare and often valuable.
- Made from carved/turned wood, ivory, bone and tusks. Ivory and exotic woods, eg rosewood, most valuable.
- Intricately carved sets more desirable.
- 'Staunton set' designed by Nathaniel Cook for Jacques & Sons in 1849 was endorsed by chess master Howard Staunton and the official set of the World Chess Federation.
- Sets should be complete and undamaged. Board not necessary. Period boxes can add value.
- Be aware of limitations on the transport of ivory.

A late 19thC Staunton-style boxwood and ebony chess set.

Glossary

Alpaca plush Very soft woolly plush made of yarn spun from the fleece of the alpaca llama.

Animated toys Any playthings that simulate lifelike movements, whether powered or activated by spring, string, flywheel, rubber band, gravity, controlled movement of sand, gyroscopic mechanism, steam electricity, or batteries.

Armature, wire Support made of wire around which a toy is constructed.

Articulated The term describing a toy connected by joints that are sufficiently loose to allow movement in any direction.

Artificial silk plush Manmade warp-pile fabric used to imitate mohair.

Artist bear A bear that is handmade by an individual artist, sometimes made as one-of-a-kind, or as a limited-edition bear.

Art-silk plush A synthetic material, originally used in the manufacture of rayon stockings and first used on teddy bears in the late 1920s.

Axle A metal rod joining two vehicle or wagon wheels.

Balance toys Toys counter-weighted with pebbles or buck shot – like roly-poly toys – that constantly return to the same starting point when set in motion. Also includes early tin toys that were weighted above or below the toy and, when set in motion, maintained their equilibrium.

Balance wheel Most often seen on horse-drawn vehicles, it is a small rotating or stationary wheel normally attached to a front hoof or a shaft suspended between two horses that facilitates passage across the floor.

Black light An ultraviolet light that reacts with colour pigments and chemicals used in paints and glazes. Often used to detect repainting of old toys.

Board games Games played on a specially designed card or fabric surface. The most common types of games involve players throwing dice and using counters to move across the board.

Boot-button eyes Solid wooden eyes with metal loops on back

Bound-stitched nose A wide rectangular-shaped teddy bear nose, introduced in 1938, with vertical stitching topped by a single horizontal stitch.

Burlap Coarse, canvas-like cloth.

carpet toy Toy that can be played with only on the floor – for example, a train that does not fit any standard track or a toy aeroplane that cannot fly.

Cast-iron toys Made of molten, grey, high-carbon iron, hand-poured into sand-casting moulds; usually cast in halves,

TOYS & GAMES

then mated and bolted or riveted as one. More elaborate versions incorporated interlocking nickel-plated grills, chassis, bumpers, people, and other accessories.

Celluloid The original name for Pyroxylin, an early and highly flammable form of plastic used for making toys. Invented in the US in 1869 by the Hyatt Brothers.

Clockwork mechanism Made of machined brass and steel and used to animate toys for as long as 30 minutes as interlocking gears move to uncoil a spring. Produced as a drive system for toys by clock makers beginning in 1862 and ending about 30 years later in the north-eastern US, most notably in Connecticut.

Composition An inexpensive substance made from a combination of cloth, wood, wood pulp, plaster of Paris, glue and sawdust, used for making dolls' heads, bodies, and limbs, as well as other toys, notably civilian and military figures.

Cotter pin A two-pronged metal pin that fastens the card disc joints of early bears.

Cotton plush A cheap quality plush used for teddy bears during and immediately after WWII when mohair was in short supply.

Crazing A random pattern of fine cracks in the paint of hand-enamelled toys – usually a sign that the paint is old, but it can be copied by the finest restorers.

Die-cast The term for a shape formed in a metal mould under pressure. Lead was initially used as the main ingredient of this material, but this was replaced in the UK in 1934 with mazac which was safer.

Disc joints Wooden or cardboard discs placed between the limbs and torso that allow smooth and full movement of the limbs

Distressed plush Mohair that has been treated to make it appear old.

Dralon/Draylon Acrylic fibre used in post-WWII toys

Dual plush A two-tone plush, usually with one colour tipping the ends of the mohair, used most commonly on teddy bears in the 1920s.

Eccentric wheels Wheels with a non-central axle that turn unevenly

Excelsior see wood wool.

Fairy Foam An all-in-one foam stuffing used in British teddy bears of the 1960s.

Felt Soft fabric formed from matting, rather than weaving, wool fibres.

Floor-runner A carpet train or toy that is propelled along the floor by a hand movement.

Glossary

Flywheel A mechanism used in some toys before 1914 that operated on the inertia principle, which states that a body at rest will remain at rest or if set in motion will remain in motion unless disturbed by an external force.

Friction wheel A central inertia wheel, also known as a flywheel, activated by springs in the rear wheels to set toys in motion. American toys utilized cast-iron friction wheels, European toys used cast-lead. Friction toys were popular from 1900 to the early 1930s.

"Googly" eyes Round plastic eyes with pupils that move.

Growler (tilt growler) A voice box inside a teddy bear that growls or roars when the bear is tipped.

Helvetic The manufacturer of musical movements used inside teddy bears – often mistaken as the manufacturer of the bears themselves.

Hug A group or collection of teddy bears, usually displayed in a decorative and appealing way.

Impressed Describes the method whereby a maker's mark is indented into the surface of a toy, as opposed to raised or embossed.

Incised Method whereby a maker's mark is scratched into the surface of a toy's head, as opposed to impressed.

Kapok A natural lightweight fibre made from the seed pod of a tropical tree, used for stuffing bears and often combined with wood wool.

Lead A main ingredient in some die-cast toys until 1934, most widely used in making toy figures until the 1960s.

Lithography The process introduced to toys in the 1880s by which sheets of tinplate are printed in colour in the flat before being pressed into shapes. The term also applies to paper items.

Mazac A magnesium-and-zinc-based metal alloy regularly used in the die-cast technique from 1934 onwards.

Mechanical bank A money box, usually made from cast-iron, in which the depositing of coins operated mechanical action. These were popular with both children and adults in the US after the Civil War – from 1869 to the late 19thC.

Mohair plush Fabric made originally from the fleece of angora goats but now usually a combination of wool and cotton.

Mystery action Mechanism that causes a battery-operated toy to turn to the left or right at regular intervals and to pull away from an object after a collision.

Papier-mache A combination of moulded paper pulp, a

whitening agent, and glue used during the 19thC for the construction of doll's heads and bodies and other toys.

Penny toys Inexpensive toys usually made from lithographed tinplate that have a simple push-along action. Production was mainly between 1900 and the 1930s.

Squeaker Voice-box activated by squeezing a toy (by hand pressure).

Still bank A money box which has no mechanical movement involved in the deposit of coins.

Stockinette Knitted cotton/elastic fabric.

String joints Early type of joint, joined to the torso by string.

Sub-stuffing Stuffing made from the waste of cotton manufacture, used during World War II when kapok was unavailable.

Tabbed Describes the method of joining two pieces of metal by folding a tab through a slot.

Tinplate Thin sheets of iron or steel which have been coated with a tin-based alloy.

Ultrasuede A US term for a synthetic fabric that resembles suede, used in the 1970s.

Unjointed toy Toy in which both torso and limbs are formed in one piece.

Velvet Fabric, usually silk or cotton, with soft close-cut pile.

Velveteen Cotton or mixed cotton and silk fabric, similar to velvet.

Vinyl A non-flammable and flexible yet tough form of plastic used for making dolls from the 1940s on; it had virtually replaced hard plastic by the 1950s.

Voice-box Internal mechanical device used to produce a sound and activated by squeezing or tipping a toy.

Webbed-claw stitching A distinctive style of stitching where the claws are joined together in a web pattern.

Wind-ups A term often used interchangeably for both clock and spring-driven toys. Clockwork offers superior quality and length of activation. 30 minutes as opposed to the 2 or 3 minutes for a coil or barrel-spring mechanism.

Wood wool (Excelsior) Long fine wood shavings – traditional teddy bear stuffing, often combined with kapok.

Yorkshire cloth Mohair plush woven in Yorkshire, UK, and used on UK and German bears.

Costume jewellery

CHANEL

In the 1920s, Coco Chanel (1883-1971) opened a boutique in her Paris salon dedicated to accessories and jewellery.

- Jewellery complimented her clothes' simple lines/colours.
- Faux pearls. Gold tone chains. 'Poured glass' jewellery by Maison Gripoix. Maltese Cross cuffs by Verdura.

CORO

Coro began as a New York accessories boutique in 1901. By the mid-1930s it had boutiques in most American cities.

- Double-pin Coro Duettes much sought after.
- Volume and diversity catered to most income brackets.
- Upmarket brands: Corocraft and Vendome (became subsidiary company in 1953).

HASKELL, MIRIAM (1899-1981)

Haskell opened her first costume jewellery shop in 1924 in New York.

- Company founded 1926.
- Innovative forms.
- Materials sourced from abroad. Renowned for quality of Japanese (faux) pearls. Crystal; glass beads; rose montées. During WW1: wood; feathers; plastics.
- Unusual and striking colour combinations.

HOBÉ

William Hobé set up Hobé Cie in c1927 in New York.

- Company launched on commission to produced costumes/jewellery for Ziegfeld Follies.
- Same techniques and high standards of craftsmanship found in precious jewellery.
- Vermeil, platinum, high-quality pastes, semi-precious stones.

Costume jewellery

MAZER BROTHERS

Founded by Joseph and Louis Mazer in 1927.

- Earliest pieces: classic floral, foliate, ribbon-and-bow.
- 1930s-40s: usually sterling/vermeil sterling silver.
- Joseph left in 1946. Mazer Brothers continued making jewellery until 1977.

SCHIAPARELLI, ELSA (1890-1973)

Schiaparelli established her first 'maison couture' in Paris in the early 1920s.

- In contrast with classic Chanel design, pieces were unusual and quirky. 'Shocking pink' signature colour.
- Inspired by nature, Dadaism and Surealism.
- 1949: DeRosa licensed to make her jewellery. Production ceased late 1950s.

TRIFARI

Gustavo Trifari started Trifari c1910. From 1925, it became 'T.K.F' for Trifari and his partners: Leo Krussman and Carl Fishel.

- Alfred Philippe: chief designer 1930-1968.
- Glamorous clientele. Diverse styles like Jelly Belly, figural and crown pins; patriotic jewellery.
- High quality materials.

WEISS

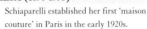

Albert Weiss left Coro in 1942 to set up his own jewellery company in New York.

- Known for rhinestone work: Austrian crystal, aurora borealis, 'black diamonds'.
- Gold/silver alloys. Sometimes enamelled/japanned. Mostly floral, foliate, figural designs.
- Marks from 1943: "Weiss", "ALBERT WEISS", "AW Co."

Glossary

Bakelite Developed in 1907 by Dr Leo Baekeland, robust plastic used in costume jewellery from the 1920s-40s, often in strong colours.

Baroque pearl A bumpy, irregular shaped pearl. Can be natural or artificial.

Base metal See pot metal.

Bib necklace A necklace with flowing beads, chains or pendants at the front which form a bib-effect.

Borealis, Aurora Iridescent rhinestones with fantasy finish, created with a polychrome metallic coating, named after the Northern Lights.

Bugle bead A long, thin, tube-shaped bead, usually glass.

Cabochon A rounded stone with a domed surface and no facets, or a paste with a flat back.

Calibré cut A stone that has been cut to follow the outline of an unusually shaped design.

Casting The process in which molten metal is poured into a mould to create a shape.

Celluloid An early plastic introduced in 1869. Highly flammable. Used for costume jewellery and hair accessories until 1920s.

Chain mail Metal fabric created from mesh of tiny metal plates or rings which are woven together.

Channel-set Setting in form of a metal channel with a rim around the edge. Rim holds the stones in place.

Christmas Tree pins Seasonal pins in the shape of Christmas trees, usually in silver or gold metal with red, green and gold beads, stones, or enamelling.

Crystal Very clear, highest quality glass, containing at least 10 per cent lead oxide.

Cultured pearls Pearls produced in controlled conditions resulting in a regular size and shape.

Demi-parure A partial matching set of two or three pieces of jewellery.

Diamanté Highly reflective, faceted crystal or glass stones.

Duette Two pins that can be clipped together as one brooch or worn separately. Well-known makers include Coro, Trifari.

En tremblant A piece of jewellery with a motif mounted on a spring, trembles when the wearer moves.

Gilding A process in which a base metal is plated with a thin layer of gold.

Pot metal A greyish base metal, made from an alloy of tin and lead. Used widely in early 20thC costume jewellery.

Parure A complete matching set of four or five pieces of jewellery, usually including a necklace, earrings, brooch/pin, and one or two bracelets.

Paste Crystal or ordinary glass with a high lead content, cut and faceted to look like a gemstone.

Pâte-de-verre A paste of crushed glass, coloured with metal oxides, then moulded and fired. Also called 'poured glass'.

Prong set A setting in which stones are held by claw-like metal prongs.

Rhinestones Faceted, highly reflective crystal or glass stones, cut to resemble gemstones. The first rhinestones were quartz stones from the river Rhine.

Rhodium A silver grey metal, unusually hard and resistant to rust. Often mistaken for silver.

Rose montée A faceted, flat-backed rhinestone, often mounted in a pierced metal cup which could then be wired to jewellery or, more frequently, clothes.

Setting The method of securing a stone in a piece of jewellery. In closed settings there is metal behind the stone. Open settings have no metal behind the stone, allowing light to shine through.

Swarovski crystals Highest-quality, brilliant-cut crystal rhinestones, produced by the Swarovski company. Much used by costume jewellery designers and couturiers.

Vermeil Sterling silver plated with gold, also called silver gilt or gold wash. Most 1940s American costume jewellery was made of vermeil sterling silver.

Pop & Disney

Rock N Roll, Elvis Presley's first UK LP, released 1956.

Pop ephemera

- There are few hard and fast rules to guide collectors of pop ephemera and it is a market in which prices fluctuate.
- Best prices are reserved for ephemera connected with giants of the pop world whose work is acknowledged to have been lasting and influential: Elvis Presley, Jimmy Hendrix and the Beatles are examples.
- Some knowledge of the rarity of a piece of ephemera is essential to avoid expensive mistakes. Unique items, such as the original artwork for a famous album cover, demonstration records and tapes, and musical instruments fetch more than autographs, posters and magazines.

- Other items of value include objects which predate the musician's fame, personal possessions, and objects connected with significant events.
- Significantly higher prices are achieved for the ephemera of artists who are no longer alive, partly because of the "legendary" characteristics they acquire and partly because this limits the amount of ephemera which is in circulation.

Disney

- Walther Elias Disney (1901-66) founded his animation studio in Hollywood in the early 1920s. Mickey Mouse was developed in 1928.
- Memorabailia from the 1930s and 40s tends to be most collectable today. Licensed products are usually more collectable.

Elton John's red platform shoes. 1970s

Posters

A 1930s-40s Mickey Mouse toothbrush holder.

However, early unlicensed items tend to be more valuable than later ones.

A James Montgomery Flagg army recruitment poster. 1917

Posters

- Virtually any poster from before WWII has a value, but it will depend on many factors including artistic

value, a famous designer, humour, social historical value, or if it had a significant impact on advertising styles.

- Very high prices are achieved by the posters of Alphonse Mucha whose work epitomized the Art Nouveau style, but works by lesser known and anonymous artists working in the same idiom are eminently collectable.

- Transport posters are a rich field for the collector, since shipping, railway and petrol companies all commissioned work of high artistic merit to promote their names.

- The value of a poster is increased if it has subsequently become famous through reproductions.

- The value or desirability of a fim poster depends on the popularity of the film, the actors in it and any cult following it may have achieved.

A Vertigo film poster, designed by Saul Bass. 1958

Lighting

■ Lighting tended to be produced in the dominant style of the period. The quality of the piece is very important. Large, highly worked pieces produced by craftsmen, made from good materials were valuable when made and are likely to still be valuable now.

An early 18thC brass chandelier with scrolling branches.

■ The earliest forms of lighting you are likely to come across are candlesticks and candelabra. These are usually made in materials that reflect the light like bronze, ormolu or gilt, and

A French Empire gilt and bronze lamp, fitted for electricity.

glass or crystal drops, which increased the reflective properties. When buying a light with drops, check that none are damaged, though it is possible to find period replacements or convincing replicas if they are.

■ Beware of reproductions, which can have a lower standard of moulding and may be made of inferior materials, for example, spelter rather than bronze. It is essential to look at period examples. Newer brass is often yellower and lighter in weight than old brass and new gilding has a brash appearance, rather than the mellow tone of old gilding. Machine work often can be seen in the rough lines made by the cutting machine.

■ Gas lighting became widespread in the early to mid-19thC, before it was superseded by electricity by the late 19thC. At this point, many fittings were

A pair of Regency bronze lustre candlesticks.

converted for electricity, which can affect desirabilty and therefore value.

■ When looking at ceramic lamps, check that they were not originally vases or jars that have been converted into lamps. For example, with a late 19thC Chinese Export vase, conversion can often enhance the value of the vase, however, a drilled early piece of Chinese porcelain can reduce in value by 70 per cent.

■ The arrival of electricity heralded the beginning of designer lighting. One of the first to focus on lamps was American Louis Comfort Tiffany, who famously designed a range of leaded glass lamps in the early 20thC. These lamps are very desirable and, therefore, often imitated and faked. Check the signature and quality of manufacture.

■ Other collectable lamp manufacturers from this era include Handel, Pairpoint.

■ 1930s Art Deco lighting is currently very popular. These were often elegant figurative lamps, or stylish geometric forms made with glass and chrome.

A pair of late 19thC US gilt-bronze three light wall sconces.

A desk lamp, by Jean Desny, glass plates on chrome base.

Index

Index

Index

Index

Acknowledgments

The publisher would like to thank everyone involved in the compilation of this book, especially the following for their kind permission to reproduce their photographs.

Anderson & Garland: 57, 70, 155, 187, 206; Albert Amor: 28, 32, 37, 38, 45, 75, 218; Ashmore & Burgess: 100; Antiques Emporium: 245; Antique Glass at Frank Dux Antiques: 90, 93; Atlantique City: 104, 105C, 228, 229, 234; Branksome Antiques: 203; Beth Adams: 54; Bath Antiquities Centre: 68; Bertoia Auctions: 236, 242, 243; Black Horse Antiques Showcase: 101, 229; Bloomsbury Auctions: 239; Brookside Antiques: 86, 105; Brunk Antiques: 144; Bonny Yankauer: 244; Cassina SPA: 155; Cheffins: 31, 37, 55, 71, 73; Clevedon Salerooms: 25, 51; Cristobal: 244, 245; David Bowden: 75; Decodame.com: 177; Doll Express: 230; Derek Roberts: 192; Donay Games: 240; Dreweatt Neate: 15, 28, 29, 34, 44, 47, 48, 57, 64, 70, 71, 74, 76, 88, 89, 90, 104, 105, 108, 110, 114, 116, 117, 123, 124, 125, 126, 127, 158, 164, 169, 190, 191, 192, 200, 204, 205, 207, 241, 250; Dorotheum: 222; David Rago Auctions: 5, 17, 18, 19, 20, 24, 36, 41, 43, 45, 46, 47, 49, 52, 53, 55, 56, 61, 63, 81, 94, 95, 96, 98, 120, 121, 149, 152, 154, 165, 167, 168, 169, 208, 220; H.Y. Duke & Son: 155; Fragile Design: 95; Auktionshaus Dr Fischer: 80, 103, 105; Freeman's: 13, 15, 16, 30, 50, 64, 68, 70, 76, 78, 79, 98, 109, 115, 117, 119, 120, 122, 124, 125, 146, 149, 150, 151, 155, 164, 165, 166, 183, 187, 188, 189, 202, 202, 203, 213, 230, 251; Guernsey's Auctions: 248; T.W. Gaze & Son: 248; Graham Cooley Collection: 99; Guest & Gray: 74; Gardiner Houlgate: 198; Galerie Maurer: 95; Galerie Marianne Heller: 62; Gorringes: 32, 38, 40, 49, 82, 215; Geoffrey Robinson: 101; Guinevere: 112; Michelle Guzy: 82; Galerie Vandermeersch: 50; Herr Auctions: 97; Galerie Hélène Fournier Guérin, 32, 39, 41, 42, 43, 44, 49, 52, 53; Harris Lindsay: 86; Imperial Half Bushel: 168; John Bull Silver: 164; James D. Julia Inc: 99; Jeanette Hayhurst Fine Glass: 87, 88, 89, 90, 93, 93, 103; John Howard: 25, 54; Jonathan Horne: 31; John Nicholson's: 29, 30, 51, 60, 62; Jean Scott Collection: 221; Auktionhaus Kaupp: 39, 47, 48, 55, 80, 198, 218; Lyon & Turnbull: 12, 13, 16, 17, 18, 18, 19, 28, 34, 35, 40, 41, 48, 50, 54, 65, 75, 96, 106, 107, 110, 111, 113, 115, 116, 118, 119, 120, 121, 122, 126, 127, 147, 150, 153, 156, 157, 158, 159, 164, 165, 169, 186, 188, 189, 191, 203, 206, 208, 209, 210, 212, 222, 223, 243, 250, 251; Law Fine Art: 37, 37, 40, 52, 55; Leanda Harwood Teddy Bears: 232, 233, 234, 235; Locke & England: 188; Mod-Girl: 244; Mark Hill Collection: 94; Mum Had That: 97; Mike Weedon: 87; Northeast Auctions: 145; Nagel: 152; Noel Barrett Antiques & Auctions Ltd: 237, 242; Norman Adams Ltd: 115; Neet-O-Rama: 239; Posteritati: 249; Partridge Fine Arts Plc: 14; Pantry & Hearth: 24, 57; Pook & Pook: 12, 14, 67, 106, 107, 113, 114, 117, 123, 125, 126, 145, 148, 156, 157, 159, 186, 202, 204, 205, 214, 215, 240; Potteries Specialist Auctions: 35; Quittenbaum: 20, 60, 94, 150; R. & G. McPherson Antiques: 70, 73; Roger Bradbury: 73; Rogers de Rin: 56, 215; Richard Gardner Antiques: 14, 147; Rick Hubbard Art Deco: 249; Roxanne Stuart: 243, 244; Sloans & Kenyon: 146; Stockspring Antiques: 50; Special Auction Services: 236, 238; Sollo:Rago Modern Auctions: 1, 20, 21, 36, 60, 61, 61, 62, 63, 63, 96, 121, 144, 147, 151, 153, 251; The Silver Fund: 167; Skinner Inc: 15, 112, 119, 214, 228; Sloans: 218; Somervale Antiques: 89, 93, 102; Swann Galleries Image Library: 249; Sworders: 34, 93, 219; Take-A-Boo Emporium: 198; Toronto Antiques Center: 67; T.C.S. Brooke: 38; Vectis Auctions: 234C, 235, 237, 238; Victoriana Dolls: 224, 228, 229, 231; Von Zezschwitz: 97, 99, 99, 148; Wallis & Wallis: 241; Wiener Kunst Auktionen - Palais Kinsky: 74, 81; Woolley & Wallis: 13, 14, 29, 30, 31, 33, 37, 39, 40, 41, 42, 45, 60, 62, 63, 66, 67, 70, 71, 75, 76, 77, 79, 88, 100, 103, 104, 168, 182, 183, 186, 220, 221, 231.